Tense Narratives

English Verbs in Context

JJ Polk

Global Touchstones

Tense Narratives

English Verbs in Context

Published by:

Global Touchstones

3183 Wilshire Blvd. NUM 196C29

Los Angeles, CA 90010, USA

FAX: +1 866 530 5692

http://www.globaltouchstones.com

Cover image credit: iStock.com/sara_winter

ISBN 978-0-692-89237-4 paperback

Typeset in LyX / LaTeX 2_ε in Baskerville.

Contents

Preface

Like numerous other lexico-grammatical aspects of the English language, the verb tense system poses special challenges for non-native speakers and learners. While the actual verb forms themselves can be learned with relative ease, correct tense usage is based on complex patterns that can be mastered only through extensive, conscientious practice involving a wide range of situations in the real world. The tenses we use should conform to the demands of our actual experience, not the other way around.

Tense Narratives: English Verbs in Context provides the learner with intensive practice activities grounded in nine non-fictional narratives. The topics in each unit have been selected to elicit students' critical thinking and problem-solving skills. The activities are designed both for the traditional classroom setting and for students who may wish to review and consolidate their existing command of English verbs through independent study.

Mastering a language, like learning a musical instrument, requires consistent, concerted practice. Both the tense-related gap-fill and post-reading questions encourage B2–C2-level students to engage with each other in discussing the reasoning behind their choice of tense. In a number of instances, several answers might be acceptable, in which case students are advised to discuss what differences or shifts in meaning, if any, might arise from the switch in tenses. Since feedback is essential in all phases of language acquisition, a comprehensive overview of the active tense system with sample sentences and an answer key have been provided in the Appendix.

Practice makes perfect!

1 Ties That Bind

Vocabulary

Match the alphabetized words in the box below with their numbered synonyms or definitions that appear beneath the box.

(A): adoption [noun] (B): afterlife [noun] (C): carpenter [noun] (D): compensate [verb] (E): convict [verb] (F): culprit [noun] (G): dictates [noun] (H): donor [noun] (I): junk food [noun] (J): linger [verb] (K): mundane [adjective] (L): point blank [adjective] (M): recipient [noun] (N): remorse [noun] (O): renowned [adjective] (P): straddle [verb] (Q): triplets [noun] (R): try [verb] (S): uncanny [adjective] (T): upbringing [noun]

1. ______ to declare someone legally guilty or culpable for a crime
2. ______ life after death
3. ______ a person who gives blood, a physical organ, or bodily tissue
4. ______ a legal process that allows an adult to become the parent of a minor child
5. ______ a person who builds or professionally works with wood or lumber
6. ______ to put on trial in a court for a crime
7. ______ a person or animal who receives blood, tissue or an organ from another
8. ______ processed food often sold in fast-food convenience stores
9. ______ famous; known to many people around the world
10. ______ direct; with no distance or nuance; unfiltered
11. ______ regret; a feeling of guilt for a wrongdoing
12. ______ strange; supernatural; weird
13. ______ three babies born to the same mother at roughly the same time
14. ______ to stay or remain in a place for a longer time
15. ______ to sit in the middle or on top of two sides
16. ______ a person who commits a crime or wrongdoing
17. ______ to make up for a failing, or to atone for a mistake or wrong
18. ______ rulings; commands; prescriptions
19. ______ everyday; ordinary
20. ______ the period or process in which a child grows up

As you read the following text, put the numbered verbs in bold CAPS into the correct form and tense. Integrate any adverbs that are provided into the correct position in the sentence. Put your responses in the corresponding numbered lines that follow the reading text. Guide question: What bonds loved ones together often for a lifetime?

Few human relationships intrigue us as much as those that exist between identical twins. Regardless of their gender, identical twins straddle the great divide between the enormously powerful influences of our socialization and upbringing on the one hand and the dictates of our genes on the other. Over the past century, researchers (**1: DOCUMENT**) numerous cases of truly uncanny coincidences between identical twins.

Those that puzzle us most, however, reveal often striking similarities between identical twins that grow up completely unknown to each other, having been separated at or shortly after birth. In their remarkable book *Identical Strangers: A Memoir of Twins Separated and Reunited,*[1] identical twin authors Paula Bernstein and Elyse Schein recounted the hidden history of their own birth and subsequent adoption through the Louise Wise Services. Thirty-five years after both women (**2: GIVE**) up for adoption, they (**3: FINALLY / REUNITE**) at an arranged coffee shop encounter in the East Village in Manhattan. Astonishingly, both women (**4: STUDY**) cinema at college and both (**5: BECOME**) writers! They also shared incredibly similar speech patterns and voices as well as their taste in music and books. Unbeknownst to either woman, they were actually victims of a scientific experiment that (**6: DESIGN**) and (**7: IMPLEMENT**) by Dr. Peter Neubauer, a renowned figure in child psychiatry. Another prominent expert in the field was Viola Bernard, who (**8: WORK**) as a consultant for the Louise Wise Services, an adoption agency, at the time the two girls were born. Bernard advocated separating all identical twins soon after birth and bringing them up in separate environments in which each would be removed from and unknown to the other. In total, three groups of identical twins and one set of triplets (**9: INVOLVE**) in the study, which ended in 1985. The view prevailed at the time (the 1960s and 1970s) that each twin could become an independent individual only if he or she (**10: ALLOW**) to develop without the influence of the identical sibling.

More than five years later, Paula Bernstein and Elyse Schein interviewed Dr. Peter Neubauer, perhaps in the hope that he might express remorse or would ask them for forgiveness; he (**11: OFFER**) them Viennese pastries instead. They (**12: STILL / WAIT**) for an apology or some indication of remorse. In a 2007 interview with National Public Radio, Paula Bernstein put it this way: "They should not have separated us. We should have grown up together. And yet, I

---

[1] Elyse Schein and Paula Bernstein, *Identical Strangers: A Memoir of Twins Separated and Reunited* (New York: Random House, 2008).

can't go back and imagine my life growing up with Elyse. That life never happened. And it is sad that as close as we are now, there's no way we can ever compensate for those 35 years."

(Twin babies. Image production credit: iStock.com/jfairone)

In terms of the unexplained similarities that often bind identical twins in a shared version of reality, the case of the "twin Jims" seems quite remarkable. Jim Lewis and Jim Springer were born in Ohio in 1940 and (**13: GROW**) up 45 miles apart in families that (**14: NOT / KNOW**) each other. The twins (**15: MEET**) in 1979 for the first time, 39 years after their birth. They subsequently became subjects in a research study that (**16: CONDUCT**) on twins. Both men had been married twice, each the first time to a wife named "Linda," and each the second time to a woman named "Betty." Both Jims had children, with sons named "James Allen"; they had also owned dogs named "Toy." Both had excelled at math in school and expressed a dislike for spelling. Both men were carpenters and had workshops in their residential garages. Each Jim (**17: SMOKE**) the same brand of cigarettes, (**18: DRIVE**) the same model of car, and perhaps most astonishingly of all, even (**19: SPEND**) their vacations at the same Florida beach—completely unbeknownst to the other! It is easy to see how identical genes predispose identical twins to develop the same medical conditions; what (**20: MYSTIFY**) researchers is how any biological basis could possibly influence the choice of a child's or a pet's name or a favored vacation destination.

Even stranger bonds (**21: REPORT**) between organ recipients and deceased donors following successful transplants. One striking instance of this phenomenon (**22: INVOLVE**) an 8-year-old girl who (**23: RECEIVE**) the heart of another 10-year-old child who (**24: BRUTALLY / MURDER**). Soon after the successful transplant, the recipient (**25: BEGIN**) having very disturbing dreams of the actual murder. In these recurring nightmares, the young girl clearly saw the face of her attacker. She later described the man in detail to the police. The authorities then (**26:**

CATCH) a man who closely (**27: MATCH**) the description the little girl (**28: GIVE**). The culprit (**29: SUBSEQUENTLY / TRY**) and (**30: CONVICT**) of the murder of the child donor.

In other more mundane instances, recipients of organs suddenly acquire new tastes in food, music, sports, and clothing, often exactly matching those of the donors. Twenty-four-year-old David Waters (**31: RECEIVE**) the heart of a teenage male, Kaden Delaney, who (**32: DIE**) suddenly in a car crash. Soon after the transplant, Mr. Waters developed a strong liking for "junk foods," in particular for "Burger Rings," a brand of chips that (**33: TASTE**) like hamburgers. Both Waters and his family (**34: BE**) at a loss to explain the changes; they (**35: KNOW**) that he (**36: NEVER / BE**) a big fan of junk food of this type before the transplant, so out of curiosity they decided to ask Kaden Delaney's family about the deceased man's food preferences. And sure enough, Delaney (**37: OFTEN / EAT**) Burger Rings as one of his favorite junk food staples.

Equally strange cases abound. In 2007, in the US state of Georgia, the heart recipient of a donor who (**38: KILL**) himself (**39: TAKE**) his own life in the exact same manner the donor had done. One study[2] of such weird coincidences reported on a 56-year-old heart recipient, "Ben," who (**40: UNDERGO**) successful transplant surgery for atherosclerosis and ischemic heart disease. The donor heart (**41: COME**) from a 34-year-old very fit police officer who (**42: SHOOT**) at point-blank range in the face. As Ben himself reported: "A few weeks after I got my heart, I began to have dreams. I would see a flash of light right in my face and my face gets real, real [sic] hot. It actually burns." The authors of the study also (**43: POINT**) out that in each of the eleven instances of donor-recipient post-transplant similarities they had analyzed, "information about the donors was specifically verified from donor family members or friends. In each case, personal changes in the recipients preceded any contact with the donor's family members or friends."

The ties that bind us often linger right up to the very end of life. Couples that (**44: LIVE**) together harmoniously for decades often (**45: DIE**) within hours of each other. Is it grief that sends the surviving mate into the afterlife in search of her loved one? Jeanette Toczko, 96, and Alexander Toczko, 95, (**46: BE**) in love with each other since they first (**47: MEET**) when they (**48: BE**) both in their early teens. They (**49: BE**) happily married for 75 years. In 2015, husband Alexander took a nasty fall and was then bed-ridden. Soon afterwards, Jeanette's own health began to deteriorate. The couple had shared their entire lives together and as they saw the end approaching, they vowed to spend their final moments together as well, at home in their own beds. On June 17, 2015, Alexander died in his wife's arms. She bade him farewell with the

---

[2] Paul Pearsall, Gary E. R. Schwartz, and Linda G. S. Russek, "Changes in Heart Transplant Recipients That Parallel the Personalities of Their Donors," *Integrative Medicine*, vol. 2, nos. 2/3 (1999): 65–72.

words: "See this is what you wanted. You died in my arms and I love you. I love you. Wait for me. I'll be there soon." Jeanette, too, (**50: KEEP**) her promise just hours later.

As the year 2016 drew to a close, Hollywood also lost one of its most beloved mother-and-daughter duos who had bonded closely together after many years of alienation. On Tuesday, December 27, Carrie Fisher, who had portrayed Princess Leia in the film classic *Star Wars*, died at UCLA Medical Center after suffering a massive heart attack on a flight from London to Los Angeles. Carries's mother, the renowned actress Debbie Reynolds, was incurably grief-stricken, and as she was making the preparations for her daughter's funeral, Ms. Reynolds suffered a massive stroke and died within hours, one day after her daughter had passed away. Ms. Reynold's last words were, "I want to be with Carrie."

In the spring of 2017, the Associated Press reported on yet another remarkable instance of couples departing the world at roughly the same time. Teresa and Isaac Vatkin of Skokie, Illinois, had been married for 69 years and they always did everything together throughout their marriage. Teresa Vatkin had been holding her husband's hand when she passed away at 00:10, April 22, 2017, in Highland Park Hospital just outside Chicago. Isaac Vatkin then died only 40 minutes later.

Use the lines below to enter the correct tense and form of the numbered verbs given in the reading text above.

1. ______________________
2. ______________________
3. ______________________
4. ______________________
5. ______________________
6. ______________________
7. ______________________
8. ______________________
9. ______________________
10. ______________________
11. ______________________
12. ______________________
13. ______________________
14. ______________________
15. ______________________
16. ______________________
17. ______________________
18. ______________________
19. ______________________
20. ______________________
21. ______________________
22. ______________________
23. ______________________
24. ______________________
25. ______________________
26. ______________________
27. ______________________
28. ______________________
29. ______________________

30. __________________________
31. __________________________
32. __________________________
33. __________________________
34. __________________________
35. __________________________
36. __________________________
37. __________________________
38. __________________________
39. __________________________
40. __________________________
41. __________________________
42. __________________________
43. __________________________
44. __________________________
45. __________________________
46. __________________________
47. __________________________
48. __________________________
49. __________________________
50. __________________________

A Vocabulary Practice

From the words given in the box at the beginning of this unit, choose an appropriate form to correctly complete the ten sentences below.

1. All the computers used in the school have been __________ by companies that have decided to update to newer models.

2. Carol __________ the highest honors and awards from our state government for her work to help homeless animals.

3. We decided to __________ two kittens and two puppies from our local animal shelter.

4. Sarah has just given birth to __________ . She's naming them Rosa, Liz, and Caroline.

5. Marx and Engels predicted that the first phase of socialism would bring about a revolution to establish the __________ of the proletariat, whose councils would then determine and implement all policies by fiat.

6. When June and Phillip first met, they realized that they had dozens of things in common — from their preferences in food, art, literature, music, and landscapes, to the way they liked to sleep in bed. It was almost as if they'd known each other all their lives, like twins separated at birth. It was really quite __________ .

7. My cousins had a very strict __________ . In fact, their parents wouldn't even permit them to own a computer or a mobile phone.

8. Heather devoted herself intensely to the study of foreign languages and music, in part to __________ for her poor mathematical skills.

9. After Midori's first performance at Carnegie Hall, everyone knew that she would one day become a __________ violinist.

10. The Nuremberg Trials succeeded in winning __________ for many of the Hitler regime's most infamous war criminals.

B True / False Questions

Based on the reading, decide if the following statements are TRUE or FALSE.

1. Both Paula Bernstein and Elyse Schein were studying film when they first met.

2. Overall, Bernstein and Schein were pleased with their meeting with Dr. Neubauer.

3. The Louise Wise adoption services is involved in the scientific study of twins.

4. Jim Lewis and Jim Springer grew up in families who lived right down the street from each other.

5. Many organ donors acquire similar tastes in food to those of their organ recipients.

6. Jim Lewis and Jim Springer frequently vacationed together at the same beach in Florida.

7. According to the Pearsall, Schwartz and Russek study, organ recipients acquired similar habits and tastes to those of their donors after meeting the donors' families.

8. Jim Lewis's and Jim Springer's families agreed never to tell the two boys that they were twins.

9. Jeanette Toczko and Alexander Toczko had been in love since the first time they saw each other when they were only in their early twenties.

10. Many devoted couples often die within hours or just a few days of each other.

C Sentence Reconstruction

Reconstruct the following TRUE sentences by putting the individual words back into their grammatically correct order. Supply appropriate punctuation as needed.

1. often when in remarkable many twins apart identical miles even exhibit grow families commonalities they separate up

____

2. met were after for adoption Bernstein/Schein years both the given first girls twins 35 up

____

3. that that to so be the could during personality psychologists her twins own many develop 1960s each believed had separated

____

4. of that to in and those their organ are some mysteriously food music donors tastes recipients acquired similar have

____

5. or to all of older each couples often who've even lives hours devoted within other die been days each other many their

____

D Discussion Questions

1. What significance does the phrase "thirty-five years" have for identical twins Bernstein and Schein?

2. Who was Viola Bernhard and what was she doing when Bernstein and Schein were born?

3. What theory prevailed among many psychologists during the 1960s and 1970s concerning the way twins and triplets should be brought up? How did this affect Bernstein and Schein? In your own view, is this theory correct? Why?

4. How did Bernstein and Schein ultimately feel about their long separation?

5. How would you explain the remarkable similarities that Jim Lewis and Jim Springer shared?

6. How would you explain the visions that repeatedly occurred in the nightmares of the 8-year-old heart recipient? Have you ever had any similar dreams or visions?

7. What could possibly explain the changes in behavior among organ recipients that mimic the behavior patterns of the donors?

8. Have you ever consciously or subconsciously adapted your own behavior to that of someone else? If so, what changes did you see in yourself and why do you believe you adapted?

9. In your view, should critically ill patients be given life-supporting organs of criminals, such as murderers or terrorists? Why?

10. Why do you believe so many very close married couples die within such a short time of each other?

2 MISSING

Vocabulary

Match the alphabetized words in the box below with their numbered synonyms or definitions that appear beneath the box.

(A): abandoned [adj] (B): ample [adj] (C): bloodhounds [n] (D): canines [n] (E): cluster [n] (F): consume [v] (G): cryptic [adj] (H): deceased [adj] (I): desert [v] (J): dissent [n] (K): extinct [adj] (L): foul play [n] (M): hang up [v] (N): law enforcement [n] (O): morning joe [n] (P): sift through [v] (Q): tenuous [adj] (R): trace [n] (S): trail [n] (T): vanish [v]

1. _____ a cup or pot of coffee in the morning
2. _____ a path
3. _____ dogs; hounds
4. _____ disagreement; noncompliance; protest
5. _____ fully sufficient in quantity
6. _____ eat up; use; devour
7. _____ a crime or illegal act
8. _____ puzzling; secret; mysterious; inexplicable
9. _____ fragile; without much substance or strength
10. _____ disappear completely
11. _____ dead
12. _____ to check through something carefully
13. _____ local or state police
14. _____ a very small amount of something
15. _____ a grouping or number of something
16. _____ to abandon or leave
17. _____ to end a phone conversation by disconnecting
18. _____ left alone; unattended; unoccupied
19. _____ dogs with an exceptionally good sense of smell
20. _____ no longer extant or alive

As you read the following text, put the numbered verbs in bold ***CAPS*** *into the correct form and tense. Integrate any adverbs that are provided into the correct position in the sentence. Put your responses in the corresponding numbered lines that follow the reading text.* Guide question: How can people, things, and time itself simply vanish?

According to the New Zealand-based news site Scoop,[1] no fewer than 4.5 million people around the world have vanished over the past 20 years! In the United States alone, approximately 2,300 Americans go missing every single day. More than 800,000 children disappear each year. In roughly 70 percent of the cases, the missing person is later found deceased, often near a body of water, such as a river or lake.

Ex-policeman David Paulides (**1: SPEND**) a number of years sifting through hundreds of such cases and (**2: WRITE**) a series of books under the title *Missing 411* on the topic. Paulides has amassed hundreds of pages that detail the events surrounding some of the most mysterious of these bizarre disappearances. Paulides hopes that one day a pattern (**3: EMERGE**) that might help law enforcement agencies prevent future occurrences. Of particular interest to author Paulides have been the hundreds of disappearances that (**4: 0CCUR**) in America's national park system, many of which date back as far as the 1800s.

Oregon's beautiful and unique Crater Lake National Park and the Cascade Range of mountains with their many alpine lakes are not only home to breathtakingly beautiful scenery, but also the site of at least 19 very strange disappearances, most of which involved men and boys. The Cascade Range of mountains stretches all the way from southern British Columbia in Canada down through Washington and Oregon into Northern California in the U.S. The earliest documented disappearance at Oregon's renowned Crater Lake involved a landscape photographer by the name of BB Bakowski. Mr. Bakowski (**5: LIVE**) in Burns, Oregon, prior to his disappearance in 1911. That year he had decided to make a winter expedition to Crater Lake to capture the extinct volcano with its deep mysterious water surrounded by a steep, snow-packed mountain range. At some point during the first week of February, 1911, the photographer had left his temporary residence in Klamath Falls for the trip north to Crater Lake, where he (**6: PLAN**) to spend three to four weeks. He had taken along ample camping supplies for approximately two months, together with a large supply of film and three cameras. Bakowski (**7: LEAVE**) instructions with friends to start looking for him if he (**8: NOT / BE**) back in a month. He (**9: NEVER / SEE**) or (**10: HEAR**) from again.

[1] "Vanishing Point: 4,432,880 Missing Persons Have Vanished In the Last Twenty Years," August 26, 2013. Full text accessed August 6, 2016: http://www.scoop.co.nz/stories/WO1308/S00441/4432880-missing-persons-vanished-in-past-20-years.htm

(Oregon's Crater Lake. Image production credit: iStock.com/JeffBanke)

A search team was sent out to locate Bakowski in March, but all they managed to find was a tarp-covered snow tunnel that Bakowski had dug, packages of exposed and unexposed film, and essentially all his supplies and clothes, but no trace of the man himself.

In August, 1965, the six-member Pankin family—Mr. and Mrs. Pankin plus sons Ted, Billy, Jimmy, and Bobby—drove from their home near Spokane, Washington, to the Deep Lake Resort just a few miles from the Canadian border. As Paulides related,[2] on the second day at the camping site, Mr. Pankin took his oldest son Ted to the lake fishing. Mrs. Pankin hiked with her other sons to a small nearby waterfall near an old abandoned logging road. Since the youngest 4-year-old son, Bobby, was barefoot and **(11: WEAR)** nothing more than his swimsuit, Mrs. Pankin instructed him to sit down in a clearing near the entrance to the trail as she and the two other sons went to look at the waterfall just a few meters away. No more than five minutes later, the mother and two sons returned to find that the youngest boy was gone. He had vanished into thin air. They began yelling his name as they searched frantically all around the area where they had left him. Nothing. They had heard nothing—no signs or sounds of other people, animals, or vehicles; no screams or indications of a struggle. And yet they were not able to find Bobby. The family immediately sought help from others who **(12: STAY)** at the resort, and dozens of people searched the entire area for Bobby. That same evening the county sheriff organized a search team with bloodhounds to track the scent of the young boy.

[2] David Paulides, *Missing 411. Unexplained Disappearances of North America That Have Never Been Solved* (North Charleston, South Carolina: Create Space, 2011) 20–23.

The dogs quickly followed the scent for almost two miles before coming to an abrupt halt at a fork in the old logging road. The dogs then refused to move; they had clearly lost the scent of Bobby. No trace of the young boy was ever found.

Union Creek, Oregon, was the site of the very unusual disappearance in 1998 of experienced hunter Robert M. Bobo, who was 36 years old at the time he went missing. Mr. Bobo had set up his campsite on October 2, in full anticipation of the yearly hunting season, which began the following morning. Mr. Bobo was known among friends and family for the cap he always (**13: WEAR**); he essentially never (**14: TAKE**) it off except to sleep or shower. The last time anyone saw Robert was around 21:00 on the night of October 2. According to Paulides's account of the case, at the opening of hunting season the next morning, one of Robert's friends arrived at the campsite only to find that Robert (**15: VANISH**). His things including all his clothes and rifles—and his famous cap—were all found in the tent the hunter (**16: SET**) up the night before, but Robert himself was nowhere to be found. No one ever saw the man again.

In October of 2006, young 8-year-old Samuel Boehlke went missing as he and his father were traveling around Crater Lake to see the majestic scenery. Kenneth Boehlke and his son Samuel had driven from their home in Portland, Oregon, to a cabin they had rented at Diamond Lake resort just north of Crater Lake. The next day, father and son headed south to Crater Lake and proceeded to drive around the lake, following the winding Volcanic Legacy Scenic Byway in a counterclockwise direction. After lunch at the Crater Lake Lodge, they made their way around to the eastern side of the lake. According to Paulides, at about 16:00 the two then stopped the car at a parking lot on the west side of the scenic road. Young Samuel quickly darted across the road with his father trailing behind to look at an interesting rock formation. Samuel circled around the large rocks, scampered over a nearby mound and then disappeared into a wooded area. The father followed quickly behind but had lost sight of his son. He repeatedly yelled out the young boy's name, to no avail. Since he (**17: NOT / GET**) any cell phone reception, the father went back to the road to get help from other motorists who (**18: DRIVE**) by. Within hours, dozens of park officials were actively looking for the lost young boy. The search continued for over a month and included over 200 people, helicopters, and search dogs. According to Paulides, the police canines had displayed a very peculiar response. After they (**19: GIVE**) the initial scent of the boy, the dogs ran to the wall of the parking lot in the direction of the lake itself, not across the road as the father (**20: REPORT**) in recounting the boy's last movements. As in hundreds of other cases, no one ever saw the boy again.

David Paulides reports that the largest single cluster of strange disappearances in the United States (**21: OCCUR**) at California's beautiful Yosemite National Park and in the surrounding

Sierra Nevada mountain range. Like the instances that (**22: REPORT**) in other parts of the world, many of the disappearances simply defy explanation. Of the 33 disappearances cited in this region in Paulides's *Missing 411*, few are as puzzling as that of 14-year-old Stacey Arras in July, 1981. Stacey and her father had signed up for a horseback trek through the High Sierra Camps inside of Yosemite. After their first midday meal near Upper Cathedral Lake, the group made its way southwest to Sunrise High Sierra Camp, where they had planned to spend the night. Although saddle-sore from the long ride, Stacey Arras decided to join Gerald Stuart, an older member of the group, on a 2.4 km hike to Sunrise Lakes at an elevation of approximately 2450 m.

(California's Yosemite Valley. Image production credit: iStock.com/garytog)

The area itself offers breathtaking vistas of craggy peaks and many small alpine lakes, all surrounded by granite outcroppings and groves of trees. The hike proved to be more strenuous than either Stacey or Gerald (**23: ANTICIPATE**), so Gerald informed Stacey that he needed to take a break to rest for a few minutes. Stacey walked on ahead toward Sunrise Lake, into nowhere. A nine-day search ensued, which turned up absolutely no clues as to what might have happened to young Stacey Arras.

Numerous highways across the U.S. outback have also been scenes of unexplained disappearances. In 2011, 86-year-old Patrick Carnes and his trusted dog Lucky were driving back home to Reno, Nevada, from a trip to Ohio where they had been visiting family. At around 21:00 on April 13, Carnes was on the last 550 km leg of the 3300 km trip when he (**24: PULL**) over by a Nevada Highway Patrol officer for an illegal lane change. The officer's dash-cam recorded

Carnes as saying "I'll never drive at night again." Carnes was given a warning and sent on his way. Carnes's green 2005 Subaru Forester (**25: SPOT**) nine hours later, parked near Interstate 80, Exit 205, near Winnemucca, Nevada. After the car had been in the same unmoved position for two days, the police (**26: BRING**) in to investigate. Both Patrick and Lucky (**27: VANISH**) without a trace. An extensive search of the entire area turned up nothing. The investigation revealed that the car itself (**28: WORK**) perfectly with enough gas, and all of Patrick Carnes's possessions appeared to be untouched. The police (**29: NOT / FIND**) any unusual fingerprints or any indication of a struggle of any kind. Even Carnes's roadmap was still in the front seat. Very odd, however, was the fact that the car was on the south side of Interstate 80 facing east, the opposite direction Mr. Carnes (**30: HEAD**) before he vanished. Patrick Carnes had also made a rather cryptic statement to the Nevada patrol officer: "I'm only following him because he's going to Elko." The dash-cam in the officer's patrol car recorded the mysterious passing of a large transport truck to which Carnes may have been referring. Exactly who the other driver was and how he and Carnes could have met remain a mystery.

Most unsettling about the Carnes case is the fact that five years earlier, 62-year-old Judith Casida had disappeared at the exact same location under nearly identical circumstances. The native resident of Cold Springs, Nevada, had written her husband a note on Valentine's Day 2006 that she was leaving him. No one knows what her final destination was, but her 1991 Mazda truck was found abandoned at Exit 205, in the exact same location where Patrick Carnes disappeared five years later. Ms. Casida's vehicle, too, was working perfectly when it was checked. No trace of Judith Casida herself, however, was ever found.

Unlike the numerous disappearances in many wilderness areas in the US and Canada, those along the interstate highway system most likely involve foul play that (**31: PERPETRATE**) by one person or even a group of people. Those that disappear in the depths of North America's extensive forests are clearly being snatched by something quite unknown. Human beings simply (**32: NOT / VANISH**) into thin air without a trace in the middle of nowhere, dozens of kilometers from the nearest human settlements.

As astonishing as it might seem, strange disappearances are not restricted to individuals, but in several cases have involved entire groups of people. During the Japanese occupation of China, 2,988 armed Chinese soldiers reportedly vanished from the face of the earth on December 10, 1937. As part of Colonel Li Fu Xien's plan to hold off the Japanese forces from entering the Chinese capital of Nanking, the Chinese troops were strategically positioned along a battle line of just over three kilometers in length to prevent the Japanese from taking a key bridge that spanned the mighty Yangtze River. On December 11, Colonel Xien's assistants (**33: REPORT**) that they (**34: LOSE**) all contact with the large Chinese troop contingent. The Chinese chain of command sent out a search team to investigate and discovered that, indeed, all the soldiers had simply vanished. All their weapons, including heavy artillery, were in position, ready and waiting to be fired—but the troops themselves had gone.

A number of hypotheses surfaced as to what might have happened to the troops. Some conjectured that they had simply deserted, but in retrospect, it seems very unlikely that anyone could have persuaded all 2,988 men to desert as if they were acting as a single person with no dissent, especially in light of the fact that they chose not to carry their weapons for protection. In addition, no unaccounted troops were ever seen or reported by neighboring villagers or townspeople.

After the war (**35: BE**) over, Chinese officials closely examined the official records that (**36: LEAVE**) behind by the Japanese occupiers. The Chinese thought that the Japanese may have taken the men prisoner that fateful night. But there was no indication whatsoever that the Japanese were even aware of the existence of the Chinese troops or their disappearance. Nothing indicated that any fighting or struggles had taken place. And to this day, no plausible explanation or account has ever been given for the mysterious disappearance of China's soldiers that December night.

In addition to individuals and groups of people, objects both big and small sometimes vanish without a trace. In July of 1988, the Soviet Union launched reconnaissance probes Phobos 1 and Phobos 2 toward Mars and its two moons, Phobos and Deimos. A programming error in August caused Phobos 1 to become disoriented with respect to the sun, shifting its solar panels away from their only source of energy. Ground control thus lost all communication with the satellite on September 2, 1988. Phobos 2 was initially a much greater success and the probe assumed its intended orbit around the red planet in January 1989. It managed to send back more than 30 relatively clear images of Mars and its moons before setting its sights on Phobos, the larger of the Martian moons, as its final destination. Its mission also included the deployment of two landers onto the Martian moon.

Several of the images captured by the Soviet satellite stood out as being very peculiar. One series of images taken of the surface of Mars just south of the planetary equator revealed a shadow of enormous size moving across the terrain. The elliptical shadow, captured by both optical and infrared cameras, was clearly defined against the background of the Martian surface and was characterized by very sharp ends. It appeared to be in an orbit between Phobos 2 and the planet's surface. The dimensions of the cylindrical object (**37: ESTIMATE**) to be approximately 1.5 km in diameter and 20 km in length! The spooky identity of the shadow on the Martian surface and the enormous cylinder captured as Phobos 2's last image remain a complete mystery even today. Phobos 2 vanished without a trace shortly after capturing its last image.

Unexplained disappearances of objects are not restricted to large exotic satellites. Perfectly sane people (**38: RELATE**) how within a clearly defined space such as a bedroom a significant object strangely vanishes into thin air without a trace. Extensive searches over weeks or even months frequently fail to turn up any sign of the missing items. When all logical explanations—the covert actions of a thief; absent-mindedness; a simple misplacement—(**39: ELIMINATE**), one must accept the seemingly impossible. It's almost as if there are tiny black holes that inhabit our space and they frequently decide to wreak havoc on our own personal lives by swallowing up things and people.

As difficult as it is to imagine how people and things could simply vanish without a trace, it puzzles us even more when what goes missing is time itself. And yet, hundreds of instances of just such a phenomenon have been reported in many countries.

In an online posting dated May 16, 2013, Jason Offutt related how the space-time continuum itself shifted one Friday evening while he (**40: DRIVE**) home from his night shift at the newspaper.[3] Mr. Offutt (**41: SET**) the cruise control in his car to 55 mph just before he began his drive home to Orrick, Missouri. As he passed a road sign saying "Orrick–5 miles," he heard the opening chords of his all-time favorite Rolling Stones hit, "Gimme Shelter," which he knew to have a length of 4 minutes and 37 seconds—just enough time, he thought, to get home and hear the song in its entirety. Since he (**42: MAKE**) the same trip many times before, he basically knew every turn in the road inside-out. Except for one strange thing: a sudden pull on the car engine indicated to him that the car (**43: TRY**) to maintain constant speed as it went uphill. But Mr. Offutt knew there were no other hills to climb on his way home. Offutt slowed down as he tried to re-orient himself to the unusual terrain. He went over two more hills before he arrived at the lights of a Jehovah's Witness church he was very familiar with. Now comes the strange part: the church was five miles on the other side of his intended turnoff! And: his favorite song (**44: STILL / PLAY**) on the radio with another whole minute to go! In other words, doing the math, he had somehow accomplished the impossible: he had driven ten miles in three minutes at 55 mph. Something was clearly wrong somewhere.

A number of readers to the blog site commented on Offutt's eerie account with similar bizarre reports of their own. Two IT specialists who both described themselves as thoroughly rational,

[3] The accounts reported here can be read in full at: http://mysteriousuniverse.org/2013/05/strange-cases-of-missing-time/

no-nonsense types with no hankering whatsoever for any form of the supernatural recounted how quite inexplicably time had gone missing from their daily routines. A Mr. Rolko Jando related an event that he described as "the most disturbing thing" that had ever happened to him. He (**45: DRIVE**) back home one evening with his girlfriend who was sitting in the passenger's seat. Shortly after they came to a road sign which said that they were 35 km from his hometown, one of Mr. Jando's friends rang him on his cell phone and asked how much longer he (**46: BE**). Mr. Jando responded that he was about half an hour away, tops. Mr. Jando said that he (**47: HARDLY / HANG**) up the phone when it rang again. It was the same friend asking the same question again—where he was and why he wasn't back yet. "I'm like, 'what's wrong with you? We just talked!'" His friend corrected him, saying that that had been an hour and a half earlier! Mr. Jando checked his call logs and determined that, indeed, the friend was telling the truth. He then asked his girlfriend when she thought the first call from the friend had been made, and she, too, said that it had been "just now."

Equally eerie, as he reported, was the fact that he then passed another road sign informing them that they were 30 km from their hometown. Since there were no turnoffs or any other means of exiting the highway, the driver and his girlfriend were somehow missing an hour and a half of time and (**48: DRIVE**) only 5 km! *Where were they and what were they doing during this entire time?*

Another reader, an electrical engineer who identified herself as Jamalayka Jamalaya, recalled how approximately 60 minutes inexplicably disappeared from the daily routine she (**49: GO**) through for more than three years. She normally left her home at almost exactly 8:00 every morning for the 36-mile drive into work. She said that she routinely drove in the 70-mph range, but faster on days when she happened to be in a bad mood. On the particular Tuesday morning in question, traffic had even been lighter than usual because of school holidays. When Ms. Jamalaya arrived at her workplace, she immediately noticed that all the parking spaces were already taken. Ms. Jamalaya looked at both the clock in her sports car and the watch on her wrist—both said it was 9:35. She had not stopped anywhere along the way into work; she had left her house at almost exactly 8:00 for the 36-mile drive; and she had encountered virtually no traffic on the way. And, importantly, she (**50: DRIVE**) in her normal 60–70 mph speed range. The trip that had normally taken her only 40 minutes had somehow magically consumed a full 95 minutes of her time. What's more, if we assume the low end of her speed range, in that length of time, she should have been approximately 90 miles away from home as opposed to the 36-mile distance to her office. Ms. Jamalaya simply cannot account for the extra 45 to 60 minutes that were missing from her drive.

What does it say about our tenuous relationship to the space-time continuum we live in when people, objects, and even time itself simply vanish?

Use the lines below to enter the correct tense and form of the numbered verbs given in the reading text above.

1. ______________ 26. ______________
2. ______________ 27. ______________
3. ______________ 28. ______________
4. ______________ 29. ______________
5. ______________ 30. ______________
6. ______________ 31. ______________
7. ______________ 32. ______________
8. ______________ 33. ______________
9. ______________ 34. ______________
10. ______________ 35. ______________
11. ______________ 36. ______________
12. ______________ 37. ______________
13. ______________ 38. ______________
14. ______________ 39. ______________
15. ______________ 40. ______________
16. ______________ 41. ______________
17. ______________ 42. ______________
18. ______________ 43. ______________
19. ______________ 44. ______________
20. ______________ 45. ______________
21. ______________ 46. ______________
22. ______________ 47. ______________
23. ______________ 48. ______________
24. ______________ 49. ______________
25. ______________ 50. ______________

A Vocabulary Practice

From the words given in the box at the beginning of this unit, choose an appropriate form to correctly complete the ten sentences below.

1. After providing only a very __________ argument in his own defense, the accused thief was sentenced to prison.

2. __________ have worked for years trying to decipher the meaning of the Voynich Manuscript, but the book, its language and meaning remain a complete mystery.

3. Uncontrolled growth in human populations and the rapid encroachment of human settlements into traditional wildlife regions will inevitably lead to the __________ of thousands of species.

4. There is __________ evidence to show that alcohol and drug abuse frequently contribute to domestic violence.

5. Many military codes of conduct around the world provide for the imprisonment of__________.

6. Forensic analysts found __________ of deadly toxins in two of the victims.

7. After the 1986 nuclear catastrophe at Chernobyl, Ukraine, the entire affected region had to be __________.

8. Zones of specialized industries tend to group in __________, such as Silicon Valley for technology giants and the Boston area for biotech research.

9. Economists have consistently seen the highest rice __________ rates in India and China.

10. I know my friend was mad at me because she just __________ without saying "Good-bye."

B True / False Questions

Based on the reading, decide if the following statements are TRUE or FALSE.

1. Russian satellites Phobos 1 and Phobos 2 had similar mission goals.

2. Approximately 30 percent of the people who go missing each year are found again.

3. The strange disappearances of hikers and climbers in America's wilderness areas go back approximately 50 years.

4. Experts believe that most of those who've gone missing near Crater Lake actually drowned in the lake.

5. Mrs. Pankin and her two sons Billy and Jimmy had heard the youngest son scream just before he vanished.

6. The police believed that young Bobby Pankin was taken by a car that was passing by.

7. The friends of Robert Bobo discovered signs of a struggle near the area where Robert disappeared.

8. The bloodhounds that were assigned to track young Samuel Boehlke followed the scent of the boy for more than two miles in the same direction that the father had said his young son had taken.

9. The elliptical shadow photographed on the surface of Mars has been explained as the actual shadow of Phobos 2 itself.

10. The largest number of documented unusual disappearances in the USA are clustered around Crater Lake, Oregon.

C Sentence Reconstruction

Reconstruct the following TRUE sentences by putting the individual words back into their grammatically correct order. Supply appropriate punctuation as needed.

1. to to of is in the disappearances California unexplained Paulides Yosemite according Park largest National author home cluster single

____

2. was of the of a that a recorded person Lake disappearance named Oregon's first photographer from Crater Bakowski

____

3. of the in to are areas follow America's tracking vanished persons wilderness often scent unable who've dogs

____

4. the of the of in that was police disappearance play Nevada suspected work Patrick Carnes northern foul strongly

____

5. a of to for are experienced who've people time hours period account often missing several over unable their whereabouts or actions

____

D Discussion Questions

1. In your own view, why do so many people go missing in National Parks?

2. Based on your own knowledge, what other regions in the world have been sites of strange disappearances?

3. Why does it seem unlikely that those who've disappeared were taken by wild animals?

4. A great many of those who've disappeared simply vanished into thin air. In your view, what could explain the fact that their bodies have never been found?

5. In your own words, explain the phrase *missing time*.

6. How and why is the case of Mr. Patrick Carnes and his dog Lucky, who disappeared near Interstate 80 in Nevada, different from the disappearances of hikers in the Cascade Range?

7. In your own words, recount the missing time experiences related by Mr. Offutt in Missouri and by the IT professional and his girlfriend. How do they differ from each other? In what ways are they the same?

8. In your own view, what might explain the missing time experiences described in this unit? What objections might someone raise against your explanation?

9. What do you believe happened to Phobos 2? Explain your thinking.

10. If you had to go camping for two weeks in a wilderness area of the American West, how would you prepare and how would you protect yourself?

3 Unexplained Aerial Phenomena

Vocabulary

Match the alphabetized words in the box below with their numbered synonyms or definitions that appear beneath the box.

(A): affirmative [adj] (B): altitude [n] (C): beams [n] (D): bright [adj] (E): flight plan [n] (F): hover [v] (G): intentions [n] (H): intruders [n] (I): minuscule [adj] (J): negative [adj] (K): novel [adj] (L): performance envelope [n] (M): pick up [v] (N): prowess [n] (O): sketch [v] (P): stack [v] (Q): switch [v] (R): take place [v] (S): track [v] (T): walk of life [n]

1. _____ a written record of the flight path a pilot intends to use
2. _____ invaders; uninvited people who trespass
3. _____ elevation; height
4. _____ to place one on top of another vertically
5. _____ extremely small; tiny
6. _____ to draw an image by hand
7. _____ the position, status, or station a person holds in society
8. _____ to detect
9. _____ *NO* in military or aviation language
10. _____ advanced or superior skills
11. _____ positive; *YES* in military or aviation language
12. _____ the purposes, goals, or aims a person has
13. _____ rays of light
14. _____ to hang suspended in the air in one place
15. _____ reflecting a large amount of light
16. _____ to change or exchange
17. _____ to follow on radar or by means of location detecting instruments
18. _____ new
19. _____ the entire set of abilities of an aircraft
20. _____ to occur; happen

As you read the following text, put the numbered verbs in bold ***CAPS*** *into the correct form and tense. Integrate any adverbs that are provided into the correct position in the sentence. Put your responses in the corresponding numbered lines that follow the reading text.* Guide question: Do UFOs exist?

In 1989 and 1990, thousands of people from all walks of life witnessed a spectacular array of aerial phenomena that simply cannot (**1: EXPLAIN**) on the basis of our current knowledge. Over a period of almost two years, in villages and towns across eastern Belgium near the German border, thousands of people including police and military officers (**2: CALL**) their local authorities to notify them of bizarre objects that (**3: HOVER**) over both towns and farms. Many of the objects appeared to be perfect isosceles triangles with sides of approximately 35 m. Many of the triangles were equipped with intense illumination devices at each corner and in the exact center. For unknown reasons and with unknown intentions, they directed intense beams of light of various colors at spots on the ground. Many of the witnesses became frightened because of the strange flight characteristics of the objects.

On the night of November 29, 1989, calls started streaming in to local authorities from hundreds of people. As the numbers of calls continued to grow, local authorities contacted the Belgian air force to see if they (**4: SOMEHOW / INVOLVE**). Since the Belgian air force knew nothing of the incidents themselves, they in turn inquired with both the American air force and NATO command whether either or both might be involved in unusual military maneuvers of some kind.

Colonel Wilfried de Brouwer of the Belgian military said that no authority he had contacted had any information about the objects. All the authorities stated categorically that they (**5: NOT / CONDUCT**) any test flights with experimental aircraft or prototypes. On November 12, 2007, Major General de Brouwer recounted for an audience at the National Press Club in Washington, D.C., the major findings of the investigations that (**6: CONDUCT**) by the Belgian air force at the time:

> I could confirm that no flights of stealth aircraft or any other experimental aircraft took place in the airspace of Belgium. In addition, the civil aviation authorities confirmed that no flight plan had been introduced. This implied that the reported objects or craft committed an infraction against the existing aviation rules. The Belgian air force tried to identify the alleged intruders and on three occasions launched F16 aircraft. On one occasion, two F16s registered rapid changes in

> speed and altitude which were well outside the performance envelope of existing aircraft.[1]

Professor Emile Schweicher of the Belgian Royal Military Academy analyzed the data recorded by four different radar facilities, all of which (**7: TRACK**) the objects from different locations. He confirmed that the data demonstrated quite conclusively that the objects performed with inexplicable prowess and agility. The objects were able to accelerate from 50 knots to more than 1000 knots in just seconds. They climbed to an altitude of more than 10,000 m and then descended to a height of just a few hundred meters in just seconds as well, and even at great speeds turned at right angles—aeronautical feats that are simply impossible with our laws of mechanics. Even when they (**8: HOVER**) still over the ground, whatever system (**9: PROPEL**) them (**10: DO**) so completely silently without any detectable changes to the surrounding air columns. Professor Schweicher summed up the conclusions of most of those who (**11: WITNESS**) or investigated the phenomenon this way: "I'm going to be fired by my colleagues, but I think that extraterrestrial intelligence is very highly likely."

A particularly noteworthy encounter involving unidentified flying or aeronautical objects (**12: GAIN**) international attention in 1986. On November 17, Japan Air Lines flight 1628 (**13: CARRY**) a shipment of French wine from Paris to Tokyo. After a layover in Iceland, JAL 1628 (**14: BEGIN**) the final leg of its journey back to Tokyo. Captain Kenju Terauchi, an exceptionally experienced former fighter pilot, (**15: FLY**) the Boeing 747 cargo plane. Terauchi (**16: ACCOMPANY**) by his co-pilot, Takanori Tamefuji and highly skilled flight engineer, Yoshio Tsukuba.

Until shortly after flight 1628 entered the northeastern corner of Alaska, everything (**17: GO**) exactly as planned. The plane (**18: FLY**) on auto-pilot at a cruising altitude of 11,000 m and an airspeed of approximately 900 km/h. The pilot (**19: INFORM**) by the air traffic control authorities in Anchorage to head in the direction of Talkeetna, Alaska, for the flight over the Aleutians and then on toward Japan.

Captain Terauchi (**20: DO**) exactly as he (**21: TELL**). But soon afterward the pilot and his crew (**22: NOTICE**) something very strange. Approximately 600 m beneath the 747 on the left side of the plane were two unusual objects, which the crew originally assumed were American military aircraft. The objects (**23: TRACK**) JAL 1628's flight path and speed exactly. The objects (**24: CONTINUE**) this tracking pattern for approximately ten minutes. And then suddenly, in a feat

[1] See Major General Wilfried De Brouwer, "The UAP Wave over Belgium" in Leslie Kean, *UFOs—General, Pilots, and Government Officials Go on the Record* (New York: Harmony Books, 2010) 24–40.

of extraordinary agility, the objects completely (**25: REARRANGE**) themselves into a stacked flying position about 200 m right in front of the 747! Captain Terauchi said that the objects "became dazzlingly bright."

It was then that the crew (**26: KNOW**) they (**27: SEE**) something completely novel in aviation history. First of all the objects had a very strange appearance. Both consisted of a very dark central core from which multiple rows of illumination of some type (**28: EMANATE**). The objects (**29: EMIT**) a type of flame in irregular patterns, but they appeared capable of controlling all the movements by this means. Second, the movements themselves defied the conventions of aviation mechanics: "The thing was flying as if there was no such thing as gravity. It sped up, then stopped, then flew at our speed, in our direction, so that to us it [appeared to be] standing still. The next instant it changed course."[2]

Within just under ten seconds the UFO (**30: JUMP**) from being approximately eight miles ahead of JAL 1628 to a position roughly seven miles behind the 747. Captain Terauchi decided to alert Anchorage air traffic control to the situation and to ask whether the authorities there (**31: KNOW**) of any aircraft in the vicinity where the objects (**32: SIGHT**). According to the translated and transcribed interviews with the flight crew, they (**33: REMAIN**) in radio contact with Anchorage for more than 30 minutes, but they (**34: FORCE**) to switch to a different radio frequency because of heavy unexplained static.

At around 17:25, the military's Elmendorf Regional Operational Control Center reported that they (**35: PICK**) up signals on their radar screens from unidentified objects. The Anchorage Air Traffic Control Center (AARTCC) and the military's facility at Elmendorf (ROCC) (**36: SEEK**) mutual clarification and confirmation for what their radar screens (**37: TELL**) them.

As flight 1628 (**38: NEAR**) Fairbanks, the captain reported something astonishing: the appearance of what his crew firmly believed was "the mothership": "We must run away quickly! Anchorage Center. The JAL 1628 is requesting a change of course to right 45 degrees."

At approximately 17:25, the ROCC radar officer said: "I don't know if it's erroneous or whatever, but…"

The AARTCC answered: "Negative, it's not erroneous. I want you to keep a good track on there and if you pick up a [transponder signal], verify that you do not have any [military] aircraft operating in that area."

---

[2] For a detailed account of JAL 1628's encounter with the unidentified flying object see Dr. Bruce Maccabee, "The Fantastic Flight of JAL 1628," accessed August 11, 2016 at: http://brumac.8k.com/JAL1628/JL1628.html. See also John J. Callahan, "The FAA Investigates a UFO Event 'That Never Happened'," in Leslie Kean, *UFOs–Generals, Pilots, and Government Officials Go on the Record* (New York: Harmony Books, 2010) 222–229, and the UFO Casebook file, accessed August 11, 2016 at: http://www.ufocasebook.com/jal1628surfaces.html

The ROCC responded: "That is affirmative. We do not have anybody up there right now. Can you give me the position of the primary you're receiving?" AARTCC: "I'm picking up a primary approximately 50 miles southeast. But it's right in front of the (JAL 1628)."

Both military and civilian radars (**39: PICK**) up the same objects that the crew of JAL 1628 (**40: SEE**) in real time. A "primary" (**41: BE**) a radar return signal that (**42: NOT / HAVE**) a corresponding electronic transponder identification code. JAL 1628 then promptly flew into Anchorage at 18:20. Weeks after the incident, the crew (**43: INTERVIEW**) about their unusual experience. Captain Terauchi actually sketched the "mothership" which he (**44: DESCRIBE**) as the size of a large aircraft carrier, in relationship to his 747. The plane (**45: LOOK**) positively minuscule by comparison. The enormity of the unidentified flying object that (**46: TAIL**) JAL 1628 caused the crew to fear for their lives. On landing in Anchorage, the crew appeared to be visibly shaken.

The tapes of the 31-minute radar tracking of these mysterious objects (**47: LATER / ANALYZE**) at the highest levels of the U.S. government. John Callahan, former chief of the Accidents, Evaluations, and Investigations Division of the Federal Aviation Administration (FAA) in Washington, D.C., led the investigation. Callahan later stated for the record: "When they asked me what I thought, I told them that it looked like we had a UFO that was up there. [...] My guess is, eh, because of the way it was—that it's not part of the military's operation anymore—that it was a UFO. But who do you tell that you were involved in a UFO incident without them looking at you like 'you ain't wrapped too tight!'? As far as I'm concerned, I saw a UFO chase a Japanese 747 across the sky for over half an hour on radar."

The extraordinary flight characteristics that (**48: DISPLAY**) by all UFOs and their highly elusive nature (**49: LIKELY / MEAN**) that they (**50: REMAIN**) a mystery for many years to come.

Use the lines below to enter the correct tense and form of the numbered verbs given in the reading text above.

1. ____________	9. ____________
2. ____________	10. ____________
3. ____________	11. ____________
4. ____________	12. ____________
5. ____________	13. ____________
6. ____________	14. ____________
7. ____________	15. ____________
8. ____________	16. ____________

17. ______________________
18. ______________________
19. ______________________
20. ______________________
21. ______________________
22. ______________________
23. ______________________
24. ______________________
25. ______________________
26. ______________________
27. ______________________
28. ______________________
29. ______________________
30. ______________________
31. ______________________
32. ______________________
33. ______________________
34. ______________________
35. ______________________
36. ______________________
37. ______________________
38. ______________________
39. ______________________
40. ______________________
41. ______________________
42. ______________________
43. ______________________
44. ______________________
45. ______________________
46. ______________________
47. ______________________
48. ______________________
49. ______________________
50. ______________________

A Vocabulary Practice

From the words given in the box at the beginning of this unit, choose an appropriate form to correctly complete the ten sentences below.

1. Residents in the area have been warned to be on the lookout for nighttime __________ who appear to be breaking into wealthier houses.

2. I'm sure she didn't __________ to hurt the boy's feelings, but he was clearly quite taken aback by her comments.

3. The company has developed a __________, fairly inexpensive method to purify stagnant water using only gravity.

4. At 5,000 m, most people will suffer from some form of __________ sickness unless they have been slowly acclimated to the new elevation.

5. The U.S. Geological Survey recently reported that they had been __________ signals of increased volcanic and seismic activity under Yellowstone National Park.

6. The evening sun was shining so __________ through my windshield that I had to pull over and wait for it to go down.

7. The post-wedding reception actually had people from all __________ represented, from diplomats and college professors to plumbers, taxi drivers and prison guards.

8. I knew it was an accident waiting to happen because the girl had __________ more than 20 books on top of each other, just ready and waiting to topple over.

9. Bloodhounds are incredibly good at tracking even the most __________ trace of a person's body odor.

10. All the political fundraising events __________ at the International Congress Hall.

B True / False Questions

Based on the reading, decide if the following statements are TRUE or FALSE.

1. The only people who saw the UFOs over Belgium in 1989 and 1990 were civilians.

2. Belgian military experts demonstrated that the UFOs were in fact experimental prototypes of the American air force.

3. The flight characteristics of the UFOs seen over Belgium were comparable to those of advanced military aircraft today.

4. The UFOs reported by Japan Airlines flight 1628 in 1986 were seen by both the cockpit crew and all the passengers.

5. JAL 1628 first spotted the UFOs just after take-off from Iceland.

6. The UFOs reported by JAL 1628 could not be detected by either civilian or military radar.

7. James Callahan of the U.S. government's Federal Aviation Administration believed that JAL 1628 had indeed witnessed genuine UFOs.

8. Professor Emile Schweicher of Belgium believed the UFOs seen over his country were operated by extraterrestrial intelligence.

9. The crew of JAL 1628 were all very experienced and were thus able to calmly report on everything they had observed.

10. Captain Terauchi actually drew pictures of the UFOs he claimed JAL 1628 had observed.

C Sentence Reconstruction

Reconstruct the following TRUE sentences by putting the individual words back into their grammatically correct order. Supply appropriate punctuation as needed.

1. the by the all of of life seen Belgium people UFOs were from members over large in walks 1980s late

____

2. were Belgian the sources military by tracked UFOs radar multiple

____

3. of of in that the of the three plane large shaken flight UFOs over tracked crew Alaska November appearance by their 1986 visibly JAL 1628 were

____

4. and by by the confirmed both UFOs radar civilian were JAL 1628 military reported

____

5. for be by that the that engineered fighter UFOs humanly Belgian witnessed pilots were flight would aircraft patterns displayed impossible

____

D Discussion Questions

1. In your view, what were the people of Belgium actually seeing in 1989–1990? Explain your thinking.

2. Given the ability to fake photographic evidence, how would it ever be possible to confirm the existence of real UFOs? What kind of evidence would suffice?

3. What interest would governments have in keeping the existence of UFOs secret, if we assumed that our governments knew positively that such extraterrestrial phenomena existed?

4. In your own words, recount the events surrounding the flight of JAL 1628.

5. If you could sit down face-to-face with Capt. Terauchi, what questions would you ask him or his crew? Do you trust the account given by the crew of JAL 1628? Why or why not?

6. If you ever saw a flying object that you were convinced was a UFO, how would you react? Would you tell others about the experience?

7. If we assume that the objects over Belgium and the objects observed by the crew of JAL 1628 were genuine extraterrestrial craft of some kind, what do you believe their purpose was?

8. A number of commercial airlines explicitly forbid their pilots from talking publicly about UFOs they might experience. Why, in your view, would airlines ever adopt such policies?

9. If we again assume that many of the UFOs being reported worldwide are in fact really of extraterrestrial origin, how should governments respond? Why? Explain your thinking.

10. If you ever came face-to-face with beings from a different solar system, how would you react? Would you try to communicate with them? And if so, what would you want them to know?

4 Off-Limits

Vocabulary

Match the alphabetized words in the box below with their numbered synonyms or definitions that appear beneath the box.

(A): black ops [n] (B): civilians [n] (C): classified [adj] (D): compliance [n] (E): disclosure [n] (F): disposal [n] (G): extraterrestrial [adj] (H): fiction [n] (I): lawsuit [n] (J): negligent [adj] (K): off-limits [adj] (L): pertinent [adj] (M): plaintiffs [n] (N): resolutely [adv] (O): restricted [adj] (P): select [adj] (Q): surroundings [n] (R): suspense [n] (S): unmarked [adj] (T): unpaved [adj]

1. _____ something that is not factual; imagined; created in the mind
2. _____ restricted; not to be entered
3. _____ non-military people
4. _____ the act of getting rid of something
5. _____ lacking care or concern; careless
6. _____ of an origin outside the earth
7. _____ parties that file a lawsuit against another party
8. _____ a legal proceeding in which one party seeks justice from another for a crime or illegal act
9. _____ of a particular, distinguished quality
10. _____ without an asphalt or concrete surface
11. _____ with limited access only for those with permission
12. _____ excited uncertainty; apprehension
13. _____ data or information that is secret or sensitive
14. _____ the public revelation of material, information or data
15. _____ highly secret military operations
16. _____ obedience to a command or order; adherence to rules
17. _____ with determination and firmness
18. _____ relevant to; germane to
19. _____ the environment of a place
20. _____ without identifying letters, numbers, or symbols

As you read the following text, put the numbered verbs in bold ***CAPS*** *into the correct form and tense. Integrate any adverbs that are provided into the correct position in the sentence. Put your responses in the corresponding numbered lines that follow the reading text.* Guide question: Why would a government deny the existence of something real?

Approximately 130 km north-northwest of downtown Las Vegas, Nevada, (**1: LIE**) one of the most secret and heavily guarded areas outside of North Korea. The general public first became aware of the region, which (**2: BECOME**) known as *Area 51,* through Soviet satellite images that (**3: RELEASE**) in the 1980s.

For years the U.S. government and its military branches resolutely (**4: DENY**) even the existence of such a secretive place that (**5: KEEP**) completely off-limits to all but a very select few. Older maps (**6: IDENTIFY**) the area in question as "Groom Lake," and the region was, and still is widely believed to be an advanced testing facility for "black ops" projects that (**7: CONDUCT**) by various branches of the U.S. military.

Area 51 is but a small part of an entire restricted complex which (**8: RUN**) by the U.S. Air Force. This includes the Nellis Air Force Range, the Tonopah Test Ranges, the Nevada Test Site, and the Tonopah Bombing Range. Personnel who work at Area 51 (**9: FLY**) into the region by a special courier service on unmarked airplanes whose windows have been blackened out.

In 1995, a lawsuit brought by five unnamed civilians and the families of two deceased men against both the Environmental Protection Agency of the USA and the U.S. Air Force essentially (**10: FORCE**) the government's hand. The plaintiffs in the suit, who (**11: REPRESENT**) by renowned law professor Jonathan Turley of George Washington University, (**12: TESTIFY**) that they (**13: SERIOUSLY / SICK**) by chemicals they had been exposed to while they (**14: WORK**) at Area 51. The widows of two of the men (**15: CONTEND**) that their husbands (**16: DIE**) as a result of exposure to those chemicals. The lawsuit claimed both that the U.S. Air Force (**17: BE**) negligent in its handling of the toxins in question, which included dibenzofuran, dioxin, and trichlorethylene, among others, and that the Environmental Protection Agency (**18: NOT / ACT**) to enforce existing laws governing the use and disposal of toxic substances.

The U.S. government responded to the lawsuit by asking the presiding judge in the U.S. District Court for Nevada not to allow any of the pertinent documents or witness testimonies to be dis-closed to the public for reasons of "national security." The judge in the case (**19: REJECT**) the government's plea. The U.S. Air Force then pulled out its heavy-handed options: it (**20: PER-SUADE**) then-president Bill Clinton to issue Presidential Determination 95-45 which exempted the U.S. government facilities at Area 51 from compliance with environmental protection laws, if compliance with these regulations led to the disclosure of classified information.

The U.S. government (**21: GUARD**) Area 51 and its secrets extraordinarily well. The entire surroundings are equipped with infrared heat sensors, motion detectors, sound receptors, CCTV cameras, and ground sensors so sensitive that they can detect mice as they (**22: SCURRY**) across the desert floor. Only a couple of unpaved and unmarked dry desert roads (**23: LEAD**) the curious into the mountain range, beyond which the nation's top secrets are kept. Visitors who muster up enough courage to drive in for a closer look (**24: QUICKLY / MEET**) by armed guards, and if need be, by helicopters equipped with missiles. Signs (**25: WARN**) intruders that Deadly Force Is Authorized.

(Area 51 Perimeter. Image production credit: iStock.com/sipaphoto)

The extreme secrecy surrounding Area 51 (**26: LEAD**) to all kinds of speculation. A man by the name of Bob Lazar has claimed that he (**27: ONCE / EMPLOY**) at Area 51 on a project to reverse-engineer extraterrestrial aircraft that the U.S. government (**28: SOMEHOW / OBTAIN**).

Very little information about Area 51 can (**29: CORROBORATE**) or verified simply because of the secrecy that enshrouds the area. This, in turn, has led to the quasi-cult status the area enjoys in film, fiction, and television. It contains all the material that good suspense novels (**30: MAKE**) of.

Use the lines below to enter the correct tense and form of the numbered verbs given in the reading text above.

1. ____________	7. ____________
2. ____________	8. ____________
3. ____________	9. ____________
4. ____________	10. ____________
5. ____________	11. ____________
6. ____________	12. ____________

13. ______________________ 22. ______________________
14. ______________________ 23. ______________________
15. ______________________ 24. ______________________
16. ______________________ 25. ______________________
17. ______________________ 26. ______________________
18. ______________________ 27. ______________________
19. ______________________ 28. ______________________
20. ______________________ 29. ______________________
21. ______________________ 30. ______________________

A Vocabulary Practice

From the words given in the box at the beginning of this unit, choose an appropriate form to correctly complete the ten sentences below.

1. Concerned citizens have now filed a __________ against the company, alleging that the firm had failed to provide the town with adequate protection against the toxic substances being used in their production lines.

2. This entire area is strictly __________ for the next two weeks as experts attempt to clean up the oil spill.

3. Most company employees are refusing to __________ with the new dress code at work.

4. Visitors always feel at peace in Sedona because the entire __________ elicit serenity and a deep appreciation for the unique beauty of Nature.

5. Under U.S. law, journalistic media are not required to __________ the names of their sources.

6. Only a very __________ few individuals have ever been invited to a private audience with the British monarch.

7. The wars in Afghanistan and Iraq took the lives of untold thousands of innocent __________ who had no blame whatsoever for any of the events that had led up to the conflicts.

8. Mr. Jones has been fired for __________. His failure to lock the valves on the machines nearly caused a very serious accident that would have put many people at risk.

9. We feel that the arguments you've made in your defense are simply not __________ to the undeniable facts in the case.

10. Many countries are trying to __________ the flow of migrants who are attempting to settle in new regions.

B True / False Questions

Based on the reading, decide if the following statements are TRUE or FALSE.

1. The U.S. military uses Area 51 as a testing facility for experimental aircraft.

2. A number of people who claimed to have worked at Area 51 have become sick and died.

3. The American people first learned about the existence of Area 51 from congressional reports.

4. Employees at Area 51 use daily commercial flights from Las Vegas to get to work.

5. The surveillance equipment used to protect Area 51 from intruders cannot detect all types of approaching vehicles.

6. According to a lawsuit filed against the U.S. government in 1995, employees at Area 51 were exposed to highly radioactive substances.

7. Radiation levels around the perimeter of Area 51 are up to 25 times higher than the accepted normal background radiation.

8. It is the responsibility of the U.S. government's Environmental Protection Agency (EPA) to ensure that the public is not exposed to dangerous substances.

9. The Nevada U.S. District Court judge who first examined the evidence brought by plaintiffs in the 1995 lawsuit against the EPA and the U.S. Air Force rejected the basis of the lawsuit.

10. Presidential Determination 95–45, signed by Bill Clinton, established that ordinary civilians would no longer be able to sue the U.S. government for environmental violations.

C Sentence Reconstruction

Reconstruct the following TRUE sentences by putting the individual words back into their grammatically correct order. Supply appropriate punctuation as needed.

1. on the one and is places guarded Area 51 secretive most heavily government the of by operated earth U.S.

____

2. in be so or the that at airplanes classified must highly unmarked research Area 51 flown conducted on employees is work

---

3. who a at as the to of for gravely highly Force U.S. Air result employees sued former them substances exposing their toxic work became there Area 51 ill

---

4. Area 51 executive compliance president Clinton determination an from issued exempting former regulations with environmental federal

---

5. the of the is of force signs warn outside deadly visitors unwelcome authorized Area 51 that use perimeter

---

D Discussion Questions

1. Would you ever want to travel as close as possible to Area 51? Why or why not? If YES, what would you hope to see or discover?

2. What do you believe is being kept secret at Area 51? What do you think the purpose of the facility might be?

3. Should the U.S. government be required to disclose to the public the purpose of Area 51 and to reveal what goes on there? Why or why not?

4. What other areas on earth are you aware of that are also kept highly secret and off-limits to the public?

5. Under what circumstances should governments withhold important information from the public?

6. In your view, what risks do employees face who work at Area 51 and why would they ever want to take such risks?

7. As stated in the reading, a man by the name of Bob Lazar has made a few incredible, indeed quite fantastic claims about the purpose of his former employment at Area 51. How credible or believable do you think these claims are? Explain your thinking.

8. If we assume that the claims made by Bob Lazar are real, what should be the public's response?

9. In your view, is the use of deadly force justified to deter possible intruders at Area 51?

10. What other areas or facilities around the world should be kept strictly off-limits to the public? Why?

5 The Mystery of Malaysian MH370

Vocabulary

Match the alphabetized words in the box below with their numbered synonyms or definitions that appear beneath the box.

(A): adjoining [adj] (B): airspace [n] (C): avoid [v] (D): chilling [adj] (E): debris [n] (F): detection [n] (G): distress [n] (H): flight path [n] (I): head back [v] (J): hug [v] (K): incoherent [adj] (L): intentionally [adv] (M): mumble [v] (N): off course [adj] (O): static [n] (P): suicide [n] (Q): grieve [v] (R): trickle in [v] (S): vicinity [n] (T): whereabouts [n]

1. _____ deeply unsettling; frightening; very scary
2. _____ a state of emergency, hardship or adversity
3. _____ abutting; adjacent to; next to
4. _____ the taking of one's own life; killing oneself
5. _____ the location of someone or something
6. _____ noise
7. _____ the scheduled route of an airplane
8. _____ speak indistinctly or incomprehensibly
9. _____ to return or retrace a path
10. _____ parts or pieces of something that has broken up
11. _____ the air above a country that lies in its legal jurisdiction
12. _____ to experience profound sadness over the death of a loved one
13. _____ without clarity or meaning; garbled
14. _____ done purposefully; on purpose
15. _____ deviating from a planned path; erring in direction
16. _____ the act of perceiving or sensing a signal or object
17. _____ evade; prevent; escape; elude
18. _____ to arrive very slowly, one drip or drop at a time
19. _____ to stay very close to an outline, border, or other identifiable marker
20. _____ the neighborhood; a nearby location

*As you read the following text, put the numbered verbs in bold **CAPS** into the correct form and tense. Integrate any adverbs that are provided into the correct position in the sentence. Put your responses in the corresponding numbered lines that follow the reading text.* Guide question: How can large airplanes simply disappear during flight?

On March 8, 2014, at 00:42 local time, Malaysian Airlines flight MH370, a Boeing 777-200, departed Kuala Lumpur for Beijing. The plane (**1: CARRY**) 239 passengers on board, the majority of whom were Chinese nationals who (**2: RETURN**) home. The 12-member crew were all Malaysian. The planned flight to Beijing should (**3: TAKE**) approximately 5 hours and 35 minutes.

At approximately 01:00, the pilots of MH370 reported to Kuala Lumpur Area Control Center that the plane (**4: REACH**) its cruising altitude of 10,700 m. The first 30 minutes or so of the flight (**5: APPEAR**) to be completely routine. At about 01:20, Captain Zaharie Ahmad Shah acknowledged the Kuala Lumpur control tower's "send off" to their Vietnamese colleagues in Ho Chi Minh City.

> Kuala Lumpur Control Tower: "Malaysian three seven zero, contact Ho Chi Minh one two zero decimal nine. Good night."
> Captain Shah: "Good night. Malaysian three seven zero."

But Captain Shah failed to contact air traffic control in Ho Chi Minh City as flight MH370 passed briefly into Vietnamese airspace. Using the international distress frequency, another aircraft in the vicinity (**6: ATTEMPT**) to contact MH370 at the request of Ho Chi Minh City. The captain of the other flight said that they (**7: MANAGE**) to reach MH370 but that all they had heard was static and incoherent mumbling.

For some unknown reason, flight MH370 then essentially did the unthinkable: it (**8: TURN**) completely around and (**9: HEAD**) back over the Malaysian Peninsula. Since the flight (**10: HUG**) the irregular border separating Malaysia and Thailand, it managed to cross eight national borders. Malaysian aviation authorities (**11: CONTACT**) air traffic control authorities in all the adjoining countries to inquire about the whereabouts of MH370. One hour after the scheduled arrival time in Beijing, Malaysian Airlines announced that flight MH370 (**12: DISAPPEAR**), location unknown.

A vast international search effort involving many nations (**13: START**) in a frantic attempt to find MH370. The problem was where to look. The flight path that Captain Shah (**14: TAKE**) deviated completely from the planned regularly scheduled route to Beijing. Investigators simply could not understand why the plane (**15: FLY**) so far off course. It just didn't make sense, especially in light of the fact that MH370 (**16: NOT / SEND**) out any distress calls or radioed for help. The plane (**17: CROSS**) back over the Malaysian Peninsula by flying in essentially the opposite direction from its scheduled route. It then immediately (**18: MAKE**) a right hook as it (**19: APPROACH**) the southern end of Penang Island off Malaysia's western coast, crossed the Strait of Malacca, and then headed northwest over the Andaman Sea. From there, satellite data indicate that the plane (**20: FLY**) in a south-southwesterly direction across the open Indian Ocean. For some inexplicable reason the plane's main signaling devices, its transponders, either (**21: INTENTIONALLY / SWITCH**) off, or for whatever reason, had failed to function. The plane's Satellite Data Unit, however, (**22: REPEATEDLY / SEND**) out and (**23: RECEIVE**) key "pings" from orbiting satellites. This data indicated that the plane (**24: CONTINUE**) on its fatal path for nearly seven hours, when it most likely (**25: RUN**) out of fuel.

The international rescue teams from a dozen countries first (**26: SEARCH**) the waters in the Gulf of Thailand and the South China Sea, where the plane (**27: HAVE**) its last confirmed radio contact. As reports from other radar and satellite sources began trickling in, the teams (**28: FORCE**) to expand the search area first into the Strait of Malacca, then into the Andaman Sea, and finally into the remote southern Indian Ocean, at least 1500 km off the western coast of Australia. In the spring of 2016, multiple pieces of debris that leading authorities are sure (**29: BE**) part of the Boeing 777, (**30: WASH**) ashore in multiple places—on Reunion Island, on the east coat of Madagascar, and in South Africa. This lent support to the assumption that the international teams (**31: WORK**) under for two years that the plane (**32: INDEED / GO**) down in the middle of the Indian Ocean.

(Map of Malaysia. Image production credit: iStock.com/Popartic)

Sundry unanswered questions caused many sleepless nights for all those involved, in particular for the hundreds of families that (**33: BE**) left behind to grieve for their loved ones, whose remains might never (**34: FIND**). In a rather shocking interview with BBC News Magazine from April 16, 2015, experienced Australian pilot Captain Simon Hardy (**35: PROVIDE**) a truly chilling account of what he (**36: BELIEVE**) transpired on board the ill-fated aircraft. For Hardy, the key element in the puzzle is the flight path itself, and in particular the fact that the plane (**37: TURN**) sharply northwest in full view of Penang Island off the west coast of Malaysia. As Hardy noted, MH370 Captain Shah was from Penang! It was as if he wanted one last look at his birthplace and home before he (**38: HEAD**) out into the open sea, from which there was no return. And indeed, the other elements of the highly irregular flight path (**39: FIT**) in perfectly, in Hardy's view, with the intentions of a skilled pilot who (**40: WANT**) to avoid detection at all cost. In Hardy's professional assessment, Captain Shah (**41: BE**) on a suicide mission from the start and ultimately (**42: ACCOMPLISH**) his goal.

On July 22, 2016, *New York Magazine* (**43: CONFIRM**) that the Malaysian police task force that (**44: INVESTIGATE**) MH370 (**45: PROVIDE**) the magazine with "a confidential document" that clearly demonstrated that Captain Shah (**46: PRACTICE**) the same suicide mission on his home flight simulator. In the words of staff writer Jeff Wise, this document amounted to "the strongest evidence yet that Zaharie made off with the plane in a premeditated act of mass murder-suicide."[1]

Use the lines below to enter the correct tense and form of the numbered verbs given in the reading text above.

1. ______________________	11. ______________________
2. ______________________	12. ______________________
3. ______________________	13. ______________________
4. ______________________	14. ______________________
5. ______________________	15. ______________________
6. ______________________	16. ______________________
7. ______________________	17. ______________________
8. ______________________	18. ______________________
9. ______________________	19. ______________________
10. ______________________	20. ______________________
	21. ______________________

[1] Jeff Wise, "Exclusive: MH370 Pilot Flew a Suicide Route on His Home Simulator Closely Matching Final Flight," *New York Magazine,* July 22, 2016. Article accessed online July 25, 2016: http://nymag.com/daily/intelligencer/2016/07/mh370-pilot-flew-suicide-route-on-home-simulator.html

22. ______________________
23. ______________________
24. ______________________
25. ______________________
26. ______________________
27. ______________________
28. ______________________
29. ______________________
30. ______________________
31. ______________________
32. ______________________
33. ______________________
34. ______________________
35. ______________________
36. ______________________
37. ______________________
38. ______________________
39. ______________________
40. ______________________
41. ______________________
42. ______________________
43. ______________________
44. ______________________
45. ______________________
46. ______________________

A Vocabulary Practice

From the words given in the box at the beginning of this unit, choose an appropriate form to correctly complete the ten sentences below.

1. The *Titanic* sent out an SOS __________ call before she took on massive amounts of water and sank in the North Atlantic.

2. There was so much __________ on the phone that I could barely hear what my brother was saying.

3. Legend has it that the Egyptian Queen Cleopatra committed __________ by letting a poisonous snake bite her in the hand.

4. We were unable to __________ any signs or traces of gas around the premises.

5. The __________ from the buildings destroyed in the tornado was strewn over an area the size of five football fields.

6. We'd intended to go to Las Vegas for the weekend, but when we saw that the traffic was backed up for 35 km, we simply __________ home.

7. The film is a __________ account of one family's ordeal with frightening paranormal phenomena in rural England.

8. The speaker must have been on some type of heavy medication because he became almost completely __________ after only 15 minutes into his talk; people were having to guess at what the point was.

9. Visitors are advised to __________ going into poorly lit, sparsely populated areas of town after dark.

10. Stan didn't get the job for one reason only: he __________ incessantly during the interview! Everyone has told him time and time again to open his mouth and to enunciate clearly, but he simply refuses to change.

B True / False Questions

Based on the reading, decide if the following statements are TRUE or FALSE.

1. MH370 never reached its proper cruising altitude.

2. Captain Shah lied to air traffic control in Ho Chi Minh City.

3. Most of the passengers aboard MH370 were Malaysian.

4. International search teams first began looking for MH370 in the Strait of Malacca.

5. The transponders aboard MH370 were working perfectly.

6. Captain Shah was originally from Kuala Lumpur.

7. MH370 probably crashed close to Reunion Island.

8. The strongest piece of evidence that Capt. Shah may have been on a murder-suicide mission was revealed form the flight path he had practiced on his home computer.

9. The last radio contact with MH370 was over the Andaman Sea.

10. After flying back across the Malaysian Peninsula, flight MH370 made a sharp turn and headed northwest.

C Sentence Reconstruction

Reconstruct the following TRUE sentences by putting the individual words back into their grammatically correct order. Supply appropriate punctuation as needed.

1. its 20 approximately MH370 minutes takeoff altitude after reached cruising

____

2. airspace course inexplicably briefly heading Malaysian the back peninsula reversing before MH370 entered over Vietnamese southwest and

---

3. were the the heading on Chinese home nationals of MH370 majority back board passengers

---

4. and had so not its why rescue flight teams search plan far international off could understand flown MH370 scheduled

---

5. the on the of the computer taken believed home reportedly had have practiced route plane almost MH370 exact is pilot his to

---

D Discussion Questions

1. What could possibly have motivated such an experienced pilot and family father to engage in such an act?

2. What measures (including mechanical) could or should authorities have taken to prevent this tragedy?

3. In your opinion, were both the pilot and the co-pilot involved in the plan to ditch the plane in the ocean? If not, how do you imagine the scenario playing out?

4. At what point do you imagine the passengers became aware that something was seriously wrong?

5. If you had been a passenger aboard the plane, how would you have responded if you had known that the plane was possibly being hijacked?

6. How do you think the plane was able to avoid arousing suspicion among the various aviation authorities in the countries whose airspace MH370 entered or neared?

7. What can aviation authorities and governments do on a global scale to guarantee that rogue pilots are not allowed to fly?

8. What kinds of reactions do you imagine the families of the pilot and copilot had?

9. Should the grieving families who lost their loved ones bring lawsuits against Malaysian Airlines? Why or why not?

10. How could planes be better equipped to prevent something like this form happening again?

6 Mystery in the Ural Mountains

Vocabulary

Match the alphabetized words in the box below with their numbered synonyms or definitions that appear beneath the box.

(A): autopsy [n] (B): avalanche [n] (C): bring about [v] (D): bruising [n] (E): demise [n] (F): expedition [n] (G): frostbite [n] (H): gorge [n] (I): hypothermia [n] (J): infrasound [n] (K): melt [v] (L): notify [v] (M): oddly [adv] (N): paradoxical [adj] (O): perplex [v] (P): remains [n] (Q): telegram [n] (R): trek [n] (S): voluntarily [adv] (T): wilderness [n]

1. _____ self-contradictory; inconsistent; incongruous
2. _____ an extended, often arduous trip frequently made on foot
3. _____ strangely; unusually
4. _____ tissue damage resulting from long exposure to cold
5. _____ to change from a frozen solid into a liquid at a certain temperature
6. _____ a nineteenth- / twentieth-century form of electronic communication
7. _____ to puzzle, baffle, mystify, dumbfound, confuse
8. _____ to cause
9. _____ an acoustic phenomenon involving very low frequencies < 20 Hz
10. _____ the medical examination of a body to determine cause of death
11. _____ the physical body of a deceased being
12. _____ to inform someone of something
13. _____ an untamed area of nature
14. _____ a narrow canyon, ravine or gully
15. _____ damage to the skin that appears as bluish areas
16. _____ a lengthy trip involving a group or a team
17. _____ death or destruction
18. _____ dangerously low body temperature
19. _____ the sudden slip and falling cascade of a large snow mass
20. _____ done of one's own free will or volition

As you read the following text, put the numbered verbs in bold ***CAPS*** *into the correct form and tense. Integrate any adverbs that are provided into the correct position in the sentence. Put your responses in the corresponding numbered lines that follow the reading text.* Guide question: What dangers lurk in remote wilderness regions?

One of the most baffling mysteries of the twentieth century, for which no completely satisfactory explanation (**1: EVER / GIVE**), involved the uncanny demise of nine semi-professional skiers on a hiking expedition in the Ural Mountains of the former Soviet Union in 1959.

Most of the nine ski-hikers were students of the Ural Polytechnic Institute in Yekaterinburg, Russia. The original group on the expedition (**2: PLAN**) with 11 members, but one man (**3: MISS**) his train, and 21-year-old Yuri Yudin became ill just hours before the group (**4: SET**) off on its hike into the winter wilderness.

The nine-member team had first taken a train to a town called Ivdel. From there they (**5: TAKE**) a truck to the starting point of their expedition, a village called Vizhai. Their goal was to trek to Mount Otorten and then to be back in Vizhai by February 12. The leader of the team, Igor Dyatlov, for whom the area is now named, (**6: AGREE**) to send a telegram to their university sports club to notify friends and family of their safe return, which they (**7: ORIGINALLY / PLAN**) for February 12.

On January 27, the group (**8: BEGIN**) their trek toward Mount Otorten. When February 20 rolled around and the families of the team still (**9: NOT / HEAR**) a thing, the Polytechnic Institute (**10: SEND**) out a search and rescue team to bring the hikers back to safety. The search team, which included the local police and military personnel in addition to the group from Ural Polytechnic, followed essentially the same path the hikers (**11: TAKE**) and on February 26 (**12: ARRIVE**) at the campsite the hikers had set up on the side of Mount Kholat Syakhl.

All the tents (**13: STILL / STAND**) in place, but snow partially covered the tops. The entire scene perplexed the search team. For some very strange reason, several of the tents (**14: CUT**) open from the inside! Many of the clothes were left inside the tents as were the passports, cash, and other personal belongings. But oddly enough, the search team could not find any of the hikers themselves.

Then, on February 27, near a cedar tree not far from the tents, a group of soldiers and searchers (**15: DISCOVER**) the frozen bodies of Yuri Doroshenko and Yuri Krivonischenko. A short time later the search team also uncovered the bodies of team leader Igor Dyatlov and Zinaida Kolmogorova. On March 5, the searchers also discovered the body of Rustem Slobodin. It (**16: LIE**) between where Dyatlov and Kolmogorova (**17: FIND**).

Once spring arrived and temperatures increased, much of the ice and snow (**18: MELT**), which made the search much easier. And sure enough, on May 4, the search teams finally (**19: LOCATE**) the frozen remains of the rest of the team: Lyudmila Dubanina, Alexander Kolevatov, Nikolai Thibeaux-Brignolles, and Seymon Zolotariov. All were found in a narrow gorge where they apparently (**20: BUILD**) a temporary shelter of fallen tree limbs, approximately 75 m from the cedar tree where the search team (**21: FIRST / DISCOVER**) the remnants of a campfire.

The autopsies that (**22: PERFORM**) on all nine hikers revealed that seven had most likely died of hypothermia. Two of the seven, Zolotariov and Dubanina, (**23: SUFFER**) traumatic internal injuries to the head and torso. Ten of Dubanina's ribs were broken, without there being any surface indication of blunt force. One of the ribs had apparently pierced her heart. Both of her eyes as well as her tongue and the lower muscles in her mouth (**24: REMOVE**). Clotted blood found in her stomach led the forensic specialists to conclude that she (**25: STILL / BE**) alive when her tongue and part of her oral cavity were removed. Even though Slobodin's death (**26: ALSO / ATTRIBUTE**) to hypothermia, he had suffered a severe fracture to the front part of his skull, most likely from blunt force trauma. This may (**27: KNOCK**) him unconscious, which would have sped up his death from hypothermia.

(Winter in the Ural Mountains. Image production credit: iStock.com/ElenaBelozorova)

Autopsies also attributed Doroshenko's death to hypothermia, but a number of peculiarities (**28: NOT / FIT**) in with a typical death by freezing. The right side of his mouth (**29: COVER**) with a grey-colored foam of some type. He (**30: HAVE**) abrasive wounds and bruising on his right shoulder and under his armpit, and the hair on the right side of his head (**31: SINGE**). His pants were ripped with a large hole, and he (**32: WEAR**) only a single pair of wool socks, but no shoes, in sub-zero weather! In temperatures of approximately −20 °C, it's difficult to comprehend why anyone would go out voluntarily without the warmest and heaviest footwear.

For some odd reason, Yuri Krivonischenko's clothes (**33: EXHIBIT**) fairly high levels of radiation, and his body displayed visible cuts and bruises on his head, torso, and hands. The skin (**34: MISS**) from the backs of both hands, and his left legs showed burn marks as well.

Still to this day, investigators cannot understand what could possibly (**35: FORCE**) the hikers out of their tents on the night of February 2, 1959, in the dead of winter, when their tents would (**36: KEEP**) them relatively warm and protected from the elements. It's a lingering mystery why they voluntarily would have exposed themselves to almost certain death through hypothermia. Another very puzzling aspect is the fact that several hikers (**37: OBVIOUSLY / LEAVE**) their tents scantily dressed; a few of them (**38: WEAR**) only socks.

A number of hypotheses (**39: ADVANCE**) to explain what bizarre chain of events could have led to the tragic deaths of these nine young men and women who had their entire lives ahead of them with promising careers. One theory proposed by Donnie Eichar[1] holds that the geophysical terrain of the area produced an intense infrasound phenomenon that (**40: CAUSE**) the hikers to panic in the middle of the night. But this theory (**41: NOT / EXPLAIN**) the internal injuries a number of the hikers sustained or how and why a large part of Lyudmila Dubanina's oral cavity could have been removed, most likely while she (**42: BE**) still alive. The numerous injuries that (**43: SUSTAIN**) by the hikers were largely internal with very little surface bruising.

Another theory (**44: POSIT**) that the hikers may have feared an avalanche and thus fled their tents as quickly as possible to avoid being buried. But most experts have argued that the mountainside terrain where the hikers (**45: SET**) up their tents could not have generated an avalanche, especially not of the size that would have been necessary to produce the internal injuries sustained by a few of the hikers. In addition, the hikers themselves were quite experienced and would have been aware of the low likelihood of an avalanche in that area. As www.dyatlovincident.com has pointed out, there is also no geophysical evidence whatsoever that an avalanche (**46: EVER / OCCUR**) on that slope.

Still others have hypothesized that the hikers may have witnessed secret Soviet military operations and thus (**47: KILL**) so that they could never reveal whatever they might have learned. As www.dyatlovincident.com has noted, however, there were several other groups of hikers in the same area at the same time, all of whom survived. Moreover, the Soviet military had no reason to be conducting secret military maneuvers or operations in an area that is so close to towns and villages and that is frequented by so many tourists. Others have advanced the notion that the hikers (**48: ATTACK**) by UFOs and Extraterrestrials, as strange balls of light (**49: SEE**) in

---

[1] Donnie Eichar, *Dead Mountain: The Untold Story of the Dyatlov Pass Incident* (San Francisco: Chronicle Books, 2014).

the area at the same time. In fact, one of the final images captured on the camera by one of the hikers shows an odd-looking ball of light in the sky.

Some have even speculated that the hikers may have been attacked by a Yeti, the Russian version of North America's "Big Foot" or "Sasquatsch." It's important to remember, however, that searchers found no footprints other than those of the hikers themselves anywhere near the area where their bodies were found. "Paradoxical undressing" has also been cited as a possible cause of the hikers' deaths. This phenomenon is known to occur when humans are suffering from hypothermia. To preserve the body's own temperature in the most vital internal organs, the body itself restricts the flow of blood to the extremities, which can lead to frostbite. When the very mechanism that reduces the blood flow fails, blood starts to gush back into the affected areas. This then, paradoxically, can make the person feel as if her own flesh is on fire, which in turn may lead the person to remove her clothes in the dead of winter—the opposite of what she should be doing.

But as www.dyatlovincident.com has argued, this would also not account for those hikers who had made every effort to put on as many clothes as possible by taking and wearing heavier items recovered from the bodies of their already deceased friends. The theory also does not account for the disturbing injuries that were sustained by several of the members.

None of the theories that (**50: PROPOSE**) so far can account for the bizarre behavior of the nine hikers, all of whom clearly acted in a manner that ultimately brought about their own demise.

Use the lines below to enter the correct tense and form of the numbered verbs given in the reading text above.

1. ______________________________
2. ______________________________
3. ______________________________
4. ______________________________
5. ______________________________
6. ______________________________
7. ______________________________
8. ______________________________
9. ______________________________
10. ______________________________
11. ______________________________
12. ______________________________
13. ______________________________
14. ______________________________
15. ______________________________
16. ______________________________
17. ______________________________
18. ______________________________
19. ______________________________
20. ______________________________

21. ______________	36. ______________
22. ______________	37. ______________
23. ______________	38. ______________
24. ______________	39. ______________
25. ______________	40. ______________
26. ______________	41. ______________
27. ______________	42. ______________
28. ______________	43. ______________
29. ______________	44. ______________
30. ______________	45. ______________
31. ______________	46. ______________
32. ______________	47. ______________
33. ______________	48. ______________
34. ______________	49. ______________
35. ______________	50. ______________

A Vocabulary Practice

From the words given in the box at the beginning of this unit, choose an appropriate form to correctly complete the ten sentences below.

1. Ayer's Rock is located in a remote __________ region of the Australian desert.

2. Many people who take prescription blood thinners tend to __________ quite easily and hence often wear long sleeves to hide the blue or purple spots on their skin.

3. Historians are still __________ at how the Egyptians could have constructed the Great Pyramids of Giza, since the ancient Nile inhabitants had little more than primitive stone cutting tools to work with.

4. Applicants will be __________ by email of the results of their entrance exams.

5. Ben Saunders' __________ to both the North and South poles have set records for being the longest polar trips powered solely by an explorer's own legs.

6. Strong solar storms can __________ major disruptions to telecommunications and power grid systems on earth.

7. With a length of over 4000 km, a width of 200 km, and a depth of 10 km, the Valles Marineris on Mars is one of the solar system's most impressive __________ .

8. The five Great Lakes in the northern continental United States were formed through the __________ of glaciers that had covered the region when the last glacial period ended approximately 10,000 years ago.

9. Severe joint disease such as rheumatoid arthritis can cause __________ shaped fingers.

10. A group of social workers in our community is looking for __________ who would be able to go door-to-door five hours per week to check on frail senior citizens.

B True / False Questions

Based on the reading, decide if the following statements are TRUE or FALSE.

1. The search and rescue teams that were sent out to look for the nine-member hiker-skier team quickly discovered that intruders had slashed open the tents.

2. According to the autopsy reports, most of the members of the team died of blunt-force trauma to the head and from broken bones.

3. Several members of the group had had their tongues removed.

4. All the deceased members of the team were found in a deep ravine beneath a cedar tree.

5. Investigators suspected that the group were attacked by homeless miners.

6. The bodies of a few of the members exhibited strange bruising patterns.

7. Tissue collected from the nails of two of the members was that of a bear.

8. All the victims were found fully clothed.

9. All the evidence found near the camp points to the hikers' falling victim to a moderate-sized avalanche.

10. Several sets of large, unknown bootprints were found near two of the victims.

C Sentence Reconstruction

Reconstruct the following TRUE sentences by putting the individual words back into their grammatically correct order. Supply appropriate punctuation as needed.

1. the the in and in who were their nine demise all tragic experienced women Mountains men Ural and young hikers met skiers 1959

____

2. open the the of from why members their explain still team some inside Dyatlov tents investigators cut cannot own

____

3. on only the of a found with dressed their deceased scantily number feet were socks hikers

____

4. the the removed eyes of and from had female tongue hikers been one

____

5. of of that had autopsies most revealed hypothermia the died victims

____

D Discussion Questions

1. Have you ever gone on an extended expedition of the type undertaken by the nine Russians at the Dyatlov Pass? If YES, describe the trek. If NO, would you ever consider it? Where and under what circumstances? What would you want to accomplish?

2. What do you think motivated the young hikers-skiers to undertake such a trip? Do you believe they were of sound mind to do so? Explain your thinking.

3. What aspect of the narrative strikes you as being the strangest or least explicable? Why?

4. In your view, how likely is it that the group ran out of their tents in panic because they feared an avalanche was coming? Why or why not?

5. In your view, how likely is it that the group members all quarreled about something and then killed each other one by one? Why or why not?

6. In your view, how likely is it that the group was attacked by some unknown predator or by the Soviet military itself? Why or why not?

7. What do you personally believe led to the tragic death of these nine young Russians? Explain your reasoning.

8. What could the team possibly have done to prevent this tragedy?

9. Much has changed over the last 60 years in the way we hike and trek in the wilderness. How likely do you think a recurrence of this type of tragedy would be today? What provisions or precautions from our day and time could hikers take to guarantee that something of this nature doesn't happen again?

10. Which type of natural landscape—frozen tundra, barren desert, a remote, dense jungle, steep mountainous terrain—would be the most dangerous for a group of hikers? Why? Give reasons to support your view.

7 The Bilderberg Group

Vocabulary

Match the alphabetized words in the box below with their numbered synonyms or definitions that appear beneath the box.

(A): arms company [n] (B): Atlanticism [n] (C): CEO [n] (D): conglomerate [n] (E): conscientious [adj] (F): detainment [n] (G): diligent [adj] (H): disaggregation [n] (I): dominant [adj] (J) frank [adj] (K): luminary [n] (L): military-industrial complex [n] (M): nefarious [adj] (N): network [n] (O): oversight [n] (P): palatial [adj] (Q): paternalism [n] (R): protocol [n] (S): scrutiny [n] (T): venue [n]

1. _____ dedicated; dutiful; diligent; studious
2. _____ exerting or having the strongest influence on something
3. _____ the chief executive officer of a corporation
4. _____ a firm or corporation that manufactures military weapons
5. _____ keeping or holding a person in custody, usually by the police
6. _____ the treatment of subjects or subordinates as if these were children
7. _____ the place or location where an event occurs
8. _____ a star or VIP (very important person)
9. _____ having the splendid characteristics of a palace
10. _____ open, without reservation; candid; straightforward
11. _____ the supervision of an organization, department or business entity
12. _____ the process of breaking up or tearing up a whole into components
13. _____ a large multi-industry corporation often with branches in many countries
14. _____ very careful, detailed observation
15. _____ an interwoven web or complex system with many interdependent parts
16. _____ the interconnected matrix of the military and arms companies
17. _____ criminal; evil; wicked
18. _____ a movement after World War II to strengthen ties between Europe and the USA
19. _____ a set of procedures in a standardized sequence
20. _____ dedicated; conscientious; dutiful; responsible

As you read the following text, put the numbered verbs in bold ***CAPS*** *into the correct form and tense. Integrate any adverbs that are provided into the correct position in the sentence. Put your responses in the corresponding numbered lines that follow the reading text.* Guide question: Could one organization secretly control much of the world?

Every year around the end of May or the first part of June, the most powerful and secretive organization on the planet (**1: MEET**) *to chat.* Founded in 1954, the Bilderberg Group (**2: BRING**) together annually the CEOs of the most powerful multinational conglomerates with ties to the military-industrial complex, European royalty, the dominant forces in international banking and finance, the most influential figures in academic research and scholarship, as well as the prime movers and shakers in all aspects of global communications and national governments—for purposes which (**3: REMAIN**) unknown.

Since the Bilderberg Group adheres strictly to a decades-old protocol known as "Chatham House Rules," notes or recordings of the conversations (**4: NOT / ALLOW**), and no reporters (**5: ADMIT**). Not a single word or phrase of any of the discussions that (**6: TAKE**) place during the meetings may be quoted, paraphrased, or attributed outside the gathering.

The conferences (**7: USUALLY / HOLD**) in rural settings within a safe distance from larger cities. The respective venues for the superlative event, which usually consists of roughly 35 permanent members and around 100 invited guests, (**8: RESTRICT**) to Western Europe, the United States, and Canada. The name itself (**9: DERIVE**) from the fact that the very first foundation meeting back in 1954 (**10: TAKE**) place in the Hotel de Bilderberg in the Dutch city of Oosterbeek.

No one just (**11: WALK**) into a Bilderberg meeting; doing so would result in immediate arrest and detainment with an unforeseeable outcome. Meetings (**12: ORGANIZE**) strictly by invitation only, which (**13: SEND**) out several weeks in advance of the meetings themselves.

Among the 35 to 40 "permanent members" of the Bilderberg are international luminaries, such as the president of the World Bank and the director of the International Monetary Fund, as well as various members of European aristocracy. Invitations to non-permanent guests (**14: DRAW**) up by two representative members from each of the roughly 18 member states. The inner "steering committee" (**15: CHAIR**) by a distinguished permanent member who normally holds that position for a number of years. Since 2012 the chairman (**16: BE**) Henri de Castries of France. The position (**17: PREVIOUSLY / HOLD**) by: Prince Bernhard of Lippe-Biesterfeld of the Netherlands (1954–1975); Alec Douglas-Home of the UK (1977–1980); Walter Scheel of Germany (1981–1985); Eric Roll of the UK (1986–1989); Peter Carington of the UK (1990–1998); and Etienne Davignon of Belgium (1999–2011).

To keep all eyes and ears away from the discussions that take place within the elaborate, five-star palatial settings of each venue, the respective host nation (**18: PULL**) out all the stops to provide the highest levels of security, not only through a massive police force, but also through well-equipped military units. Locations of a few of the past conferences (**19: INCLUDE**):

- 2000 — Genval, Belgium
- 2001 — Gothenburg, Sweden
- 2002 — Chantilly, USA
- 2003 — Versailles, France
- 2004 — Stresa, Italy
- 2005 — Rottach-Egern, Germany
- 2006 — Ottawa, Canada
- 2007 — Istanbul, Turkey
- 2008 — Chantilly, USA
- 2009 — Vouliagmeni, Greecce
- 2010 — Sitges, Spain
- 2011 — St. Moritz, Switzerland
- 2012 — Chantilly, USA
- 2013 — Watford, England
- 2014 — Copenhagen, Denmark
- 2015 — Telfs-Buchen, Austria
- 2016 — Dresden, Germany
- 2017 — Chantilly, USA

Over the years, many conscientious and diligent journalists (**20: WONDER**) out loud why the Western mainstream media continually (**21: IGNORE**) the Bilderberg meetings. After all, if, as many Bilderberg observers have repeatedly noted, 130 Hollywood stars, or the world's best NBA players, or the most popular music artists (**22: GATHER**) "in secret" for any purpose whatsoever, reporters from every news outlet on the planet would be tripping over themselves for first-row seats to cover every moment of the event. But when the world's most powerful elite, the "masters of our earthly universe," (**23: HUDDLE**) together under the tightest security imaginable for four days, the entire event receives even less attention than the wedding announcement of your local fire chief.

But the media's strategic silence (**24: EASILY / EXPLAIN**). One of Bilderberg's "stated" purposes, in addition to the active promotion of "Atlanticism," is to offer the world's most powerful people the chance to meet face-to-face to talk candidly about cosmopolitan issues—to articulate privately, but frankly, their thoughts and concerns on a wide range of topics, without fear of being quoted or held accountable for those ideas and opinions. Privacy is thus the key phrase used repeatedly by returning members when they (**25: ASK**) about the whole purpose of the meetings.

When we (**26: CONSIDER**) that Bilderberg members own essentially all private media firms and dominate the editorial boards of every print publication in the West, it's easy to see how they consistently (**27: KEEP**) their plans and work hidden from public scrutiny.

Critics (**28: CONSISTENTLY / ARGUE**) that the Bilderberg Group and its affiliated sister organizations (**29: CREATE**) a totalitarian network of policies and activities, both legitimate and nefarious, from the active selection and promotion of key political figures into the highest positions in national governments and international consortiums, to the active manipulation of global currency exchange, commodities, and precious metals markets, to the instigation of wars and other military endeavors. What (**30: WORRY**) many critical observers of the organization is the dominating, interlocking connectedness of all members with all vital systems of Western societies, completely removed from public oversight and immune to any democratic accountability measures.

The Bilderberg Group (**31: SET**) the standard by which all social capital on a global scale can (**32: JUDGE**). Bilderberg attendees and members quite often sit on the governing boards of policy-making councils, foundations, think-tanks, multinational conglomerates, and panels with far-reaching authority. These include but are not limited to the Council on Foreign Relations, the Trilateral Commission, the Atlantic Council, the Aspen Institute, the Royal Institute for International Affairs, as well as many military-related industries and policy boards.

Charlie Skelton, who (**33: FOLLOW**) the comings and goings of Bilderbergers for a number of years for *The Guardian* (**34: DESCRIBE**) the Bilderberg framework as the ultimate "lobbying event." Skelton (**35: LIST**) just a few examples from among the vast nexus of interconnected nodes: Niall Ferguson

> appears on the Bilderberg participant list as "professor of history, Harvard University," which is true, but perhaps not quite true enough. Perhaps more tellingly [...], Ferguson is on the board of the boutique investment firm AMG, which "currently manages approximately $642 bn in assets." [...] An even better example

> is Marta Dassu, attending Bilderberg 2016 as "senior director, European affairs, Aspen Institute," which sounds a lot more dry and academic than "board member of giant Italian conglomerate, the Trevi Group" or "a director of one of the world's largest arms companies, Finmeccanica."[1]

And the list of similar instances of "conflicts of interests" (**36: GO**) on and on. Former defense ministers or other government officials routinely (**37: SIT**) on the corporate boards of defense industry conglomerates; former finance ministers and economics professors often populate the boardrooms of large investment banks. Former CEOs of financial powerhouses (**38: MAGICALLY / APPOINT**) to lead central banks. The nodes of interconnectedness paint a beautiful abstract picture of staggering complexity. Judging from all that (**39: GLEAN**) over the years about Bilderberg and from the goals of its sister organizations, one objective clearly (**40: STAND**) out above all others: the eventual disaggregation of the "sovereign" individual nation-state in favor of global governance, which (**41: ALSO / CALL**) a "new world order."[2]

Author Daniel Estulin, who literally (**42: WRITE**) the book on the Bilderberg Group, best summarized what worries many outside observers of Bilderberg: "If this is their ultimate goal—to create a single globalized marketplace, ruled by a world government (which in turn controls its courts, schools, and the people's reading habits and very thoughts), policed by a world army, financially regulated by a world bank (via a single global currency)—then we can ill afford to ignore what is happening to us and the world we live in."[3]

Of course none of the citizens in any of the countries affected by the Bilderberg nexus—arguably the entire human species—(**43: TELL**) about the world the master planners (**44: DESIGN**) and (**45: IMPLEMENT**) step-by-step. And that (**46: BE**) the very definition of paternalism. The most fundamental question of social / political philosophy reads: Who should govern and by what principles? That the governed should participate in the governing process and that the government itself should be held accountable by the governed are two fundamental tenets of liberal democracies. From what we (**47: LEARN**) about Bilderberg, however, those in power (**48: ANSWER**) these questions quite differently from those who (**49: BELIEVE**) that the citizens themselves should have a dominant voice both in deciding how they want to live,

---

[1] Charlie Skelton, "Bilderberg in Dresden: an innocent conference or conflict of interests?" in *The Guardian*, 11 June 2016. Accessed 27 July 2016 at: https://www.theguardian.com/world/2016/jun/10/bilderberg-conference-charlie-skelton-blog-academic

[2] See for instance Richard Gardner, "The Hard Road to World Order," in *Foreign Affairs*, April 1974, vol. 52, pp. 556–576, and Anne-Marie Slaughter, *A New World Order* (Princeton, NJ: Princeton University Press, 2005).

[3] Daniel Estulin, *The True Story of the Bilderberg Group* (Walterville, Oregon: TrineDay, 2009) 85–86.

under what types of laws, and in bringing about the conditions that (**50: ALLOW**) for individual freedom.

Use the lines below to enter the correct tense and form of the numbered verbs given in the reading text above.

1. ______________	26. ______________
2. ______________	27. ______________
3. ______________	28. ______________
4. ______________	29. ______________
5. ______________	30. ______________
6. ______________	31. ______________
7. ______________	32. ______________
8. ______________	33. ______________
9. ______________	34. ______________
10. ______________	35. ______________
11. ______________	36. ______________
12. ______________	37. ______________
13. ______________	38. ______________
14. ______________	39. ______________
15. ______________	40. ______________
16. ______________	41. ______________
17. ______________	42. ______________
18. ______________	43. ______________
19. ______________	44. ______________
20. ______________	45. ______________
21. ______________	46. ______________
22. ______________	47. ______________
23. ______________	48. ______________
24. ______________	49. ______________
25. ______________	50. ______________

A Vocabulary Practice

From the words given in the box at the beginning of this unit, choose an appropriate form to correctly complete the ten sentences below.

1. Our director is known for his very __________ style of speech, which is often so blunt as to border on rudeness.

2. Only the most talented musicians can ever become renowned solo performers, and even musical geniuses must practice __________ every single day.

3. This company's __________ involvement with the international drug and weapons trade reeks of criminal conduct.

4. Two speakers clearly violated __________ when they invited the king for a beer at the local bar.

5. The U.S. Food and Drug Administration has full __________ over pharmaceutical products that hit the American markets.

6. Multinational __________ like Samsung and General Electric have suppliers and subsidiaries all over the world.

7. Unfortunately, airport security officials __________ me for three hours because they thought my bassoon was a lethal weapon of some kind.

8. Companies and agencies that work with highly classified material rely heavily on __________ employees who can be trusted in all situations.

9. Frank didn't get hired for the senior executive position because he __________ the interview meeting entirely and would hardly let anyone else speak.

10. The way Mr. Williams treats his staff is sometimes very condescending. In fact, he treats all his employees as if they were small children. The entire company deeply resents his thoroughly __________ attitude.

B True / False Questions

Based on the reading, decide if the following statements are TRUE or FALSE.

1. Most people know about Bilderberg from TV news reports.

2. There are several permanent members of Bilderberg steering committees.

3. There has never been a female chairperson of Bilderberg.

4. Bilderberg never meets in non-European nations.

5. Lobbying activities are prohibited at Bilderberg.

6. Because of the large numbers of VIPs in attendance, Bilderberg usually receives top-level quasi-military protection from the host country.

7. Bilderberg meetings have been attended by at least two popes.

8. Once someone becomes a member of Bilderberg, they are never permitted to leave the group or to renounce their membership.

9. All meetings and presentations at Bilderberg are recorded by an official secretary who is trilingual.

10. Bilderberg meetings have as their goal the strengthening of the sovereignty and independence of each individual member state.

C Sentence Reconstruction

Reconstruct the following TRUE sentences by putting the individual words back into their grammatically correct order. Supply appropriate punctuation as needed.

1. of the the the and for in once men per together year some women brings meetings Bilderberg powerful most West

____

2. the the or or to that world with Bilderberg Group any strictly forbid communication press recordings adheres secrecy outside protocols

____

3. forces are the for and by guarded venues always police Bilderberg country's securely host military

____

4. the of for media Bilderberg years ignored completely existence many Western

____

5. of of of the the the or consent governed planning knowledge even nations plotting members accused Bilderberg courses and been without have

____

D Discussion Questions

1. In your view, is it legitimate for a highly powerful group such as the Bilderberg to meet in secret for the purpose of steering political decisions and developments across the globe? Why or why not?

2. If you were able to ask and have honestly answered two questions related to the global political situation today, what would those questions be?

3. In your opinion, what kinds of personalities must the permanent members of the Bilderberg steering committees have? Describe those personalities as you see them in your imagination.

4. In your view, what kinds of issues, problems, or concerns, if any, merit the intervention by a powerful global elite such as Bilderberg?

5. If you were a powerful political figure in your country, what changes would you work to enact? Why?

6. If you were a powerful political figure on the global stage, what changes would you work to enact? Why?

7. In your view, what are the most urgent problems facing your country today? Are those the same problems that existed 100 years ago?

8. In your view, what are the major obstacles to solving the problems that exist in your country?

9. In your opinion, what are the most urgent problems facing the entire world?

10. What are the major obstacles to solving those problems? Would solving these problems require groups like Bilderberg? Why or why not?

8 Our Mysterious Universe

Vocabulary

Match the alphabetized words in the box below with their numbered synonyms or definitions that appear beneath the box.

(A): continuum [n] (B): cosmologist [n] (C): crunch [n] (D): earth-shattering [adj] (E): elegance [n] (F): exponential [adj] (G): fate [n] (H): gargantuan [adj] (I): gorilla [n] (J): infinitesimal [adj] (K): monotheist [n] (L): noblest [adj] (M): outcome [n] (N): relentless [adj] (O): simultaneously [adv] (P): superlative [n] (Q): tangible [adj] (R): toss and turn [v] (S): trigger [v] (T): ultimate [adj]

1. ______ the largest of the ape species
2. ______ result; end product
3. ______ happening or existing at the same time
4. ______ an entire array or spectrum in which all parts are connected
5. ______ having or characterized by an extremely rapid increase
6. ______ momentous; of extreme importance
7. ______ extraordinarily small; minute
8. ______ to move from one side to the other repeatedly, restlessly
9. ______ the last, final, top, most extreme element or level of something
10. ______ touchable; concrete; real; solid; corporeal
11. ______ a person who studies the entire universe in all its aspects
12. ______ fineness; splendor; of a magnificent style; grandness
13. ______ destiny; an outcome or result that is destined to happen
14. ______ of or having the highest honor
15. ______ unceasing; unabated; continuous; never-ending
16. ______ a person who believes in a single god or deity
17. ______ gigantic; immense; enormous
18. ______ of the highest possible level or quality
19. ______ set off; ignite; incite; initiate
20. ______ the process or outcome of something being squashed or crushed

As you read the following text, put the numbered verbs in bold ***CAPS*** *into the correct form and tense. Integrate any adverbs that are provided into the correct position in the sentence. Put your responses in the corresponding numbered lines that follow the reading text.* Guide question: How did the universe come into being?

No mystery causes more night-time tossing and turning among cosmologists than questions about the origin and ultimate fate of the universe itself. Monotheists (**1: POSIT**) that a supreme intelligent being created the universe in the blink of an eye in what is generally called the Genesis. Most scientists (**2: HOLD**) a slightly different view, that everything around us (**3: COME**) about in one gargantuan explosion.

Most cosmologists today believe that around 14 billion years ago, just out of nowhere, the mother of all explosions (**4: GO**) off that (**5: BRING**) everything we (**6: BE**) and (**7: SEE**) into existence, including the space-time continuum itself. This superlative of all superlatives (**8: AFFECTIONATELY / KNOW**) as the *Big Bang*. According to this model, the entire universe started out as an infinitesimally small singularity that instantaneously (**9: INFLATE**) at an exponential rate. It just kept expanding and expanding until it (**10: BECOME**) the incomprehensible size of the universe we (**11: SEE**) today.

Scientists (**12: PREVIOUSLY / DEBATE**) two distinct alternative scenarios for the "end" of the universe we live in. Will space itself continue expanding forever until all stars and galaxies are so far apart that no light from any single source can ever reach any other position? Or will the universal force of gravity eventually catch up with the relentless expansion and pull everything back together into one giant cosmic crunch? If we (**13: PULL**) back on a bow string hard enough to make our tendons ache and then let loose, the arrow on the string (**14: FLY**) straight up until it's almost out of sight. But we know with certainty that at just the right moment, Nature's ultimate authority will take hold of the arrow in mid-air and with the force of a 600-pound gorilla pull it back to earth. Logic (**15: LEAD**) us to think that the universe itself might behave in the same way and that eventually gravity (**16: OVERCOME**) the forces pulling the galaxies away from each other.

The answers to this cosmic riddle (**17: BEGIN**) to fall into place back in 1998 through the study of two gigantic exploding stars called type 1a supernovae. The measurements that (**18: OBTAIN**) from these exploding stars revealed beyond doubt that the expansion of the universe (**19: PROCEED**) at an accelerated rate. Based on all that science currently (**20: KNOW**), there is simply not enough matter (mass) and hence not enough gravity to pull it all back together again. In fact, we now know that the expansion (**21: HAPPEN**) so fast that the farthest known objects from our viewpoint in space (**22: EVENTUALLY / RECEDE**) beyond the cosmic horizon; in effect, they (**23: ESCAPE**) our universe forever.

But if we go back to the beginning, to the Big Bang itself, it (**24: SEEM**) only logical to think that if in fact one "original" Big Bang (**25: START**) it all, who is to say there (**26: NOT / BE**) others, perhaps even countless others before us? Maybe there are infinite numbers of other universes out there somewhere co-existing right beside our own? The idea behind these truly fantastic assumptions is not that difficult to grasp, but trying to visualize these possibilities, let alone take them seriously, frustrates even the noblest intentions.

The first indirect formulation of the "Many Worlds" or "Multiverse" hypothesis—setting aside for a moment religious narratives found for instance in Hindu texts—(**27: DATE**) back to a talk given by Erwin Schrödinger in 1952 in Dublin. In expounding on the real-world implications of his earth-shattering equations in quantum physics, the Nobel Prize winner said that the alternative outcomes of quantum events were not exclusive events that precluded each other, but rather that all possible histories of an event "really happen simultaneously."

In Schrödinger's famous thought experiment, a closed box is set up in which the decay of a radioactive particle triggers a sensor that in turn (**28: CAUSE**) a flask of poison to break, killing the cat within the box. Schrödinger's equations (**29: IMPLY**) that the cat is both dead and alive at the same time! One leading interpretation of quantum mechanics, called the Copenhagen Interpretation, (**30: HOLD**) that it is only when an observer opens the door to the box that the "decision" (**31: MAKE**) one way or the other. In other words, only when the outside observer (**32: LOOK**) at the result does the result in fact come into being; before that, the cat is in a superimposed state of being both dead and alive. But we (**33: NOT / NEED**) to stop there. This entire experiment itself can be constructed at a higher level so that what the observer (**34: SEE**) must then be observed by yet another outside observer, potentially in an infinite succession. Accordingly, a number of physicists (**35: CONTEND**) that the higher mathematics involved in these quantum constructions forces us to conclude that all possible outcomes of all possible conditions (**36: EXIST**) simultaneously in as many worlds.

Physicist Hugh Everett expanded this notion into what later (**37: BECOME**) known as the "Many Worlds Interpretation" (MWI) of quantum mechanics, in which all possible realities exist simultaneously side by side. Renowned cosmologist Max Tegmark and esteemed physicists David Deutsch and Brian Greene (**38: CONTRIBUTE**) significantly to the multiverse theory through mathematical models of exceptional complexity and elegance. Accordingly, all possible outcomes of every possible condition and effect that could ever happen exist simultaneously in a potentially infinite number of universes. To make the thought a bit more tangible: In this world, I am the son of my parents; in another, I am alternatively the father, mother of both. In this world, I am the husband of my wife; in another, I am the wife and she is the husband. In one universe, the observer opens the box to find that the cat has died; in the other, she opens the box and is greeted with a welcoming Meow!

Use the lines below to enter the correct tense and form of the numbered verbs given in the reading text above.

1. ____________	20. ____________
2. ____________	21. ____________
3. ____________	22. ____________
4. ____________	23. ____________
5. ____________	24. ____________
6. ____________	25. ____________
7. ____________	26. ____________
8. ____________	27. ____________
9. ____________	28. ____________
10. ____________	29. ____________
11. ____________	30. ____________
12. ____________	31. ____________
13. ____________	32. ____________
14. ____________	33. ____________
15. ____________	34. ____________
16. ____________	35. ____________
17. ____________	36. ____________
18. ____________	37. ____________
19. ____________	38. ____________

A Vocabulary Practice

From the words given in the box at the beginning of this unit, choose an appropriate form to correctly complete the ten sentences below.

1. Most forms of Hinduism differ in their teachings and dogma quite significantly from the largest __________ religions—Christianity, Islam, and Judaism.

2. Bob and Alice are so deeply in love with each other that they both feel it was __________ that brought them together.

3. The grand chess master managed to defeat 15 players __________ while blindfolded the entire time.

4. The most outstanding and reputable companies are known for their __________ pursuit of perfection in the products they make as well as their first-rate customer service.

5. Under ideal conditions, certain bacterial colonies reproduce __________ and can completely overwhelm their surrounding environment.

6. Regardless of how __________ his motives may have been, his conduct was clearly wrong and unacceptable.

7. Subatomic particles are so __________ small that they can only be detected in highly sophisticated particle accelerators.

8. The __________ of our experiments won't be known before the end of the day.

9. Large submarine earthquakes have the potential to __________ devastating tsunamis.

10. Prince Charles is renowned for the __________ style he always displays in public.

B True / False Questions

Based on the reading, decide if the following statements are TRUE or FALSE.

1. The "big crunch" is described as the end result of the "Big Bang."

2. According to most scientists, the space-time continuum has always existed, for an eternity.

3. Today, most theoreticians believe the universe will continue expanding forever.

4. All evidence so far amassed indicates multiple universes are just the product of a wild human imagination.

5. The "Copenhagen Interpretation" is the only surviving version of quantum mechanics still adhered to today.

6. In quantum mechanics, an observer can influence the outcome of an experiment by merely observing the experiment.

7. According to the multiverse hypothesis, all possible outcomes of events exist consecutively in a series of possible worlds.

8. In quantum mechanics, things can be in two superimposed contradictory states at the same time.

9. Cosmologist Max Tegmark and physicist Brian Greene have now shown conclusively that quantum mechanics is no longer valid as a theory.

10. Most scientists today reject the "Many Worlds Interpretation" of quantum theory.

C Sentence Reconstruction

Reconstruct the following TRUE sentences by putting the individual words back into their grammatically correct order. Supply appropriate punctuation as needed.

1. the the the of of after an that theory expansion immediately incomprehensibly cosmological phase universe entire inflation rapid posits Big Bang entered

____

2. the an is observations rate increasing current indicate universe that expanding at

____

3. an the of to not observer according until quantum looks interpretation actually "decided" events Copenhagen mechanics are quantum

____

4. the of all simultaneously possible possible worlds exist many outcomes interpretation events in all

____

5. of of of the the a for and allows multiverses endless birth universes continual theory potentially death series

____

D Discussion Questions

1. What is your own thinking about the origins of the universe?

2. Do you personally think the multiverse theory accurately describes reality? Why or why not?

3. If you could ask and have answered any two questions about the universe, what would they be?

4. In your opinion, why do the thoughts of theoretical physicists seem so impossible or far removed from the reality we live in?

5. In your view, does theoretical physics serve any real or useful purpose? Why or why not?

6. If you could be safely transported in a time machine to an era in earth's past and return to the present unharmed, which era would you want to experience and why?

7. If it were now possible safely to explore other planets in our solar system, would you volunteer as an explorer? Why or why not? Which area of the solar system would you want to visit?

8. If human colonies now existed on Mars, would you want to visit or relocate there? Why or why not?

9. Have you ever had the feeling that you had already experienced a situation before? In your opinion, might this be an indication that you might have been in an alternative universe in which the situation actually already did occur? Why, in your opinion, is it so difficult for humans to believe in multiple universes in which there are untold numbers of copies of everything we know?

10. If you ever encountered an alternate version of yourself from a multiverse version of our own universe, how do you think you would react? What questions would you ask the alternate *you*? What would you want to know about *yourself*?

(Artist's concept of parallel universes. Image production credit: iStock.com/Sakkmesterke)

9 Apparitions

Vocabulary

Match the alphabetized words in the box below with their numbered synonyms or definitions that appear beneath the box.

(A): altar [n] (B): aperture [n] (C): birthday suit [n] (D): darkroom [n] (E): demonic [adj] (F): depth of field [n] (G): drum scanner [n] (H): emulsion [n] (I): fidelity [n] (J): ghoulish [adj] (K): grave [n] (L): haunted [adj] (M): propeller [n] (N): shutter [n] (O): sinister [adj] (P): slasher film [n] (Q): spectrum [n] (R): squadron [n] (S): substrate [n] (T): trickery [n]

1. _____ an underlying or supporting material of some type
2. _____ the area in front of a camera lens that is selected to be in or out of focus
3. _____ a raised structure in a place of worship where religious rites are performed
4. _____ a particularly violent and bloody type of movie
5. _____ a laboratory where photographic film is developed or processed in the absence of light
6. _____ the part of an airplane or ship consisting of circular blades that turn very rapidly
7. _____ a range or array of something, e.g., light waves
8. _____ in the nude
9. _____ a complex machine used to convert film images into digital pixels
10. _____ faithfulness to a person, concept, or artistic original
11. _____ a formation of piloted military aircraft
12. _____ deception
13. _____ being occupied by ghosts or spirits
14. _____ the burial plot of a person
15. _____ having the qualities of an evil spirit or entity
16. _____ the hole or opening of a photographic lens
17. _____ a chemical mixture consisting of a silver halide suspension in gelatin
18. _____ the metal blades that form the opening of a camera lens
19. _____ fiendishly ghastly or evil
20. _____ diabolical

As you read the following text, put the numbered verbs in bold ***CAPS*** *into the correct form and tense. Integrate any adverbs that are provided into the correct position in the sentence. Put your responses in the corresponding numbered lines that follow the reading text.* Guide question: Do ghosts exist?

Surprisingly large numbers of people in many countries and cultures claim to (**1: HAVE**) personal experiences of one type or other with ghosts or spirits. Reports of encounters with spirits date back centuries, and the experiences (**2: OCCUR**) in all sorts of places—from the expected cemetery and churchyard, to well-known landmarks like the *Queen Mary* and even the White House in Washington, D.C.

Some of the more compelling evidence (**3: HAND**) down over time in the form of unusual film photographs. Long before the days of megapixels and Photoshop, photographs (**4: ROUTINELY / MAKE**) on silver halide emulsions attached to celluloid strips called "film." Commercially available film was and to a limited extent (**5: STILL / SELL**) in many different types and sizes of emulsions. In addition, these celluloid substrates still fall into a fairly wide spectrum of ASA/ISO numbers that correspond to the film's sensitivity to light. Thus a film of 25 ASA (**6: EXHIBIT**) the least amount of grain, which is comparable to noise in the digital era, while a 3,600 ASA film (**7: REACT**) with much greater sensitivity to light exposure. The increased sensitivity (**8: ALLOW**) film photographers to shoot action-oriented scenes with smaller apertures to achieve greater depth of field.

In the heyday of film photography, slower films, especially monochromatic or black and white emulsions, lent themselves wonderfully to scenes that required the highest levels of fidelity and resolution. An 8x10 inch ASA 25 image that was captured with a lens of the highest caliber could easily produce an image several gigabytes in size, especially if the film was scanned with an expensive, high-resolution drum scanner.

Several film images that date back into the early twentieth century reveal quite clearly that the lens of the camera captured something that was probably not visible to the photographer at the time the film (**9: EXPOSE**). Digital images that (**10: RECORD**) on flash memory cards lend themselves easily to layer after layer of enhancement techniques. Entire scenes can (**11: ALTER**), objects deleted, colors switched, and characters or persons inserted or erased at will, with very little effort involved. While not impossible, this type of manipulation with film is extremely difficult and time consuming, and most importantly, requires advanced darkroom skills. In addition, careful analysis of an original piece of photographic film or negative will easily expose any trickery or alterations that may (**12: ATTEMPT**) with the original.

These facts add to the mystery surrounding some of the most famous images of what many believe are spirits or ghosts that have crossed over into the afterlife. One particularly haunting group photo (**13: TAKE**) of a British Royal Air Force squadron in 1919, just after the end of World War I. One of the men in the squadron, Freddy Jackson, (**14: KILL**) by an airplane propeller two days before the group photo (**15: TAKE**). Soon after the image (**16: DEVELOP**), however, the members of his squadron immediately (**17: RECOGNIZE**) Freddy! He (**18: STAND**) right beside one of his fellow servicemen in the top row of the image. It's a mystery how a man who had been killed two days earlier could show up for what was presumably the last group photo that (**19: EVER / TAKE**) of the squadron as a unit.

And then there is the equally eerie photograph that was taken by Mrs. Mabel Chinnery in 1959. Mr. and Mrs. Chinnery had been to the cemetery to visit the gravesite of Mrs. Chinnery's mother. Mrs. Chinnery had already taken several pictures of the grave itself and then decided to photograph her husband who (**20: WAIT**) patiently in the passenger seat of the family car. When the couple had the film developed, Mrs. Chinnery's mother, whose grave the daughter had just visited before snapping the picture, was clearly visible as a passenger who was perfectly positioned in the driver's-side rear seat of the car! A photographic expert was quoted as saying, "I stake my reputation on the fact that the picture is genuine."

In 1963, Reverend K. F. Lord captured a particularly ghoulish image on film at Newby Church in North Yorkshire, England. The picture was taken from in front of the altar at the church where Rev. Lord (**21: MINISTER**). He stated that there was nothing there except the altar, the cross, vases of flowers, and the background windows when he tripped the shutter on the lens. After the film was developed, however, Rev. Lord was shocked to see what looked to be a black-robed demonic presence of some kind, which many people have said closely resembles the sinister character nicknamed "Ghostface" in the Wes Craven slasher film series *Scream.*

Even the highest citadels of political power in Washington (**22: NOT / SPARE**) rumors of spirit visitations. Journalist Joan Gage reported in 2013 on a conversation she (**23: BE**) privy to during an official state dinner at the White House in honor of Brian Mulroney, who was Candian prime minister at the time.[1] Host President Ronald Reagan explained that first his son-in-law, husband of his daughter Maureen, had been frightened one evening in the Lincoln Bedroom as he (**24: WAKE**) up to find what looked like the silhouette of President Abraham Lincoln staring out the bedroom window. Maureen Reagan teased her husband repeatedly about seeing ghosts but soon changed her tune months later when she, too, (**25: WITNESS**) the exact same apparition in the same place. According to Gage, more than a dozen White House guests reported seeing the same type of apparitions. Winston Churchill is said to have been coming out of the bathroom in his birthday suit when he, too, encountered the spirit

[1] See http://www.huffingtonpost.com/joan-gage/white-house-ghosts_b_4175961.html

of Abraham Lincoln. Churchill reportedly swore he would never sleep there again. Similar apparitions (**26: REPORT**) of Dolley Madison and Abigail Adams, but President Lincoln remains the most frequently spotted guest.

The RMS *Queen Mary* also boasts of numerous tales of hauntings. Launched in 1936 as the stellar flagship of the legendary Cunard Line, the *Queen Mary* offered her guests at the time the most luxurious ocean travel experience money could buy. When World War II (**27: BREAK**) out in 1939, the ship was recommissioned for allied military purposes, carrying in total more than 800,000 military personnel to the battle lines. In July 1943, the *Queen Mary* (**28: SET**) the record for the largest number of people ever aboard a single ship at one time: 16,683.[2]

Because of the constant threats posed by German U-boats, the *Queen Mary* (**29: ALWAYS / TRAVEL**) with a military escort. In October of 1942, her escort was the much less powerful *Curacao*. Because of a tragic human error on the part of the *Curacao's* captain, the *Queen Mary* (**30: COLLIDE**) with the smaller vessel, ripping the latter into shreds and killing more than 200 men on board. The *Queen Mary* was under strict orders not to stop to rescue any of the *Curacao's* crew, and witnesses to the tragedy reported hearing the constant screams of the men who (**31: STRUGGLE**) to stay alive as the *Curacao* went down.

In 1967, the *Queen Mary* (**32: RETIRE**) to her new permanent home in Long Beach, California, where she still serves as a luxurious hotel and museum. On numerous occasions hotel staff and guests have reported seeing unexplained apparitions of men and women who (**33: DRESS**) in clothes that went out of date in the 1930s. Three areas of the ship in particular seem to be hotbeds of paranormal activity: the boiler room, which is situated a good 15 m below the surface of the water, and the two swimming pools that (**34: NOT / USE**) in decades. However, guests have also reported hearing both screams echoing through the corridors and the eerie sounds of screeching metal, as if something (**35: TEAR**) apart. One can only imagine that this is what the initial impact of the *Queen Mary* with the ill-fated *Curacao* might (**36: SOUND**) like.

Staff (**37: ALSO / STATE**) that on numerous occasions a child's wet footprints could be seen near the swimming pool and changing rooms. Staff members and guests have witnessed a slender woman dressed in a white gown who appears to pop in and out of existence in the Mauritania Room, which (**38: ORIGINALLY / DESIGN**) as a lounging area for the third-class passengers aboard. The same elegant apparition (**39: ALSO / SEE**) in many other parts of the ship including the first-class dance hall.

---

[2] Tom Ogden, *Haunted Hotels: Eerie Inns, Ghoulish Guests, and Creepy Caretakers* (Lanham, MD: Rowman and Littlefield, 2010) 40.

Dozens of guests also reported seeing a slender man dressed in black going up a staircase on the ship, only to watch him vanish at the top of the stairs. Subsequent searches of the area turned up nothing.

(Hotel Queen Mary in Long Beach, California. Image production credit: iStock.com/Phil Cardamone)

Many guests also emphatically stated that they (**40: HEAR**) children laughing and at times crying in the "third-class nursery" room, but the room in question (**41: NOT / USE**) for anything but storage for over 45 years.

Despite hundreds or even thousands of witnesses worldwide who've often given fairly detailed descriptions of unexplained apparitions they have seen, many of which appear to be recurring phenomena, no definitive proof of the actual existence of ghosts (**42: EVER / PROVIDE**), but neither have reliable explanations for the unusual phenomena. In view of this, one must ask what exactly would constitute definitive, irrefutable proof?

Most individuals who (**43: HAVE**) up-close first-hand experiences with UFOs and/or apparitions are rock-solidly convinced that what they have witnessed is absolutely real. Those who have not had such experiences (**44: LIKELY / REMAIN**) skeptical.

Use the lines below to enter the correct tense and form of the numbered verbs given in the reading text above.

1. ______________	23. ______________
2. ______________	24. ______________
3. ______________	25. ______________
4. ______________	26. ______________
5. ______________	27. ______________
6. ______________	28. ______________
7. ______________	29. ______________
8. ______________	30. ______________
9. ______________	31. ______________
10. ______________	32. ______________
11. ______________	33. ______________
12. ______________	34. ______________
13. ______________	35. ______________
14. ______________	36. ______________
15. ______________	37. ______________
16. ______________	38. ______________
17. ______________	39. ______________
18. ______________	40. ______________
19. ______________	41. ______________
20. ______________	42. ______________
21. ______________	43. ______________
22. ______________	44. ______________

A Vocabulary Practice

From the words given in the box at the beginning of this unit, choose an appropriate form to correctly complete the ten sentences below.

1. With approximately 10 million __________, Wadi Al-Salam in Najaf, Iraq, is the largest cemetery in the world.

2. Photographers who want to bring out particular features of a model often use a very shallow __________ to intentionally blur the background behind the model.

3. Infrared film __________ frequently require the use of deep red filters to accentuate the film's special characteristics.

4. Certain space telescopes have been designed to receive light exclusively in the infrared __________.

5. Applications such as Photoshop and Lightroom are what many photographers call digital __________.

6. Church attendees often receive communion, which is also known as the Holy Eucharist, in front of the __________.

7. Ultra-fast camera lenses with very wide __________ are often capable of capturing images in almost complete darkness.

8. Connoisseurs of vinyl records claim that the analogue recording and reproduction process offers much greater acoustic __________ to the original live input than digital recording and output methods do.

9. With a diameter of 9.6 meters and a weight of 131 tons, the __________ on the *Emma Maersk* container ship ranks as the largest in the world.

10. Gallium arsenide __________ are often used in the manufacture of linear and digital integrated circuits, but silicon primary layers are still used in many other types of processors.

B True / False Questions

Based on the reading, decide if the following statements are TRUE or FALSE.

1. Many people aboard the *Queen Mary* were killed when she struck the military escort ship *Curacao.*

2. Numerous overnight guests in the White House have reported seeing what appeared to be the ghosts of presidents Adams, Lincoln, and Kennedy.

3. All film photographs that putatively show images of deceased people in spirit form have proved to be fakes.

4. The image captured on film at Newby Church in England was later admitted to be of a person dressed as a character from a Wes Craven movie.

5. Images captured digitally are much easier to manipulate and edit than those recorded on film.

6. A number of guests on the *Queen Mary* have reported seeing what they believed was the ghost of Winston Churchill.

7. President Ronald Reagan was afraid to sleep in the Lincoln Bedroom in the White House.

8. Royal Air Force squadron member Freddy Jackson was killed in an accident with an airplane propeller.

9. Former Canadian Prime Minister Brian Mulroney was a frequent overnight guest of Ronald Reagan's in the White House.

10. In the photograph Mrs. Chinnery took of her husband, Mrs. Chinnery's already deceased mother appeared to be sitting in the rear seat of the car.

C Sentence Reconstruction

Reconstruct the following TRUE sentences by putting the individual words back into their grammatically correct order. Supply appropriate punctuation as needed.

1. of no the has that ever proves provided existence ghosts evidence been photographic

___

2. no the and yet can one on explain *Queen Mary* hotel seeing board guests reported staff that apparitions members have both

___

3. of to the the was error sinking human *Curacao* attributed ultimately

___

4. of the the the in Lincoln who reported night White House guests ghost seeing numerous spent have have

___

5. a be to is of of or the and can how see UFOs manipulated ghosts offer difficult always photographic ever proof images existence picture because could it edited

___

D Discussion Questions

1. Have you personally or has anyone you know ever seen an apparition that you believed was a ghost? If yes, describe that experience in as much detail as possible.

2. What legends or stories involving ghosts or haunted places exist in your culture? Describe them.

3. In your view, why do people in the UK and the USA seem to have more encounters with apparitions than do people in other parts of the world?

4. Do you personally believe in the existence of ghosts or haunted houses? Why or why not?

5. Would you accept an offer to spend three nights alone in a house or on a ship that is reportedly haunted? Why or why not? What precautions would you take if you accepted the offer?

6. In your view, how likely is it that places such as the *Queen Mary* publicize reported ghost sightings in order to attract attention and paying guests? Explain your answer.

7. If reports of hauntings and encounters with spirits are not based on real experiences, what is then their origin, in your opinion?

8. If we assumed for one minute that the numerous reports of hauntings were true, what would or could constitute proof of the existence of ghosts?

9. What places that you know of do you think are too creepy to visit? Explain why.

10. If you could have a personal encounter with one *famous* deceased person, who would that be and what questions would you want to ask?

Answer Key

Chapter 1 Ties That Bind

Vocabulary

1: E | 2: B | 3: H | 4: A | 5: C | 6: R | 7: M | 8: I | 9: O | 10: L | 11: N | 12: S | 13: Q | 14: J | 15: P | 16: F | 17: D | 18: G | 19: K | 20: T

Verb tenses

1: have demonstrated | 2: were given | 3: were finally reunited (also possible: finally reunited) | 4: had studied | 5: had become (also: became) | 6: had been designed | 7: implemented | 8: was working | 9: had been involved (also: were involved) | 10: were allowed | 11: offered | 12: are still waiting | 13: grew | 14: had not known (also: did not know) | 15: met | 16: was being conducted | 17: smoked | 18: drove | 19: spent | 20: mystifies | 21: have been reported | 22: involved |23: received (also: had received) | 24: was brutally murdered (also: had been brutally murdered) | 25: began | 26: caught | 27: matched | 28: had given | 29: was subsequently tried | 30: convicted | 31: received | 32: had died | 33: taste | 34: were |35: knew | 36: had never been | 37: had often eaten | 38: had killed | 39: took | 40: had undergone | 41: came (also: had come) | 42: had been shot | 43: pointed | 44: live (also: have lived) | 45: die | 46: had been (also: were) | 47: met | 48: were | 49: had been (also: were) | 50: kept

A Vocabulary practice

1: donated | 2: received | 3: adopt | 4: triplets | 5: dictatorship | 6: uncanny | 7: upbringing | 8: compensate | 9: renowned | 10: convictions

B True / false questions

1: False | 2: False | 3: False | 4: False | 5: False | 6: False | 7: False | 8: False | 9: False | 10: True

C Sentence reconstruction

1. Identical twins often exhibit remarkable commonalities even when they grow up in separate families many miles apart.

2. The Bernstein / Schein twins first met 35 years after both girls were given up for adoption.

3. During the 1960s many psychologists believed that twins had to be separated so that each could develop her own personality.

4. Some organ recipients have mysteriously acquired tastes in food and music that are similar to those of their donors.

5. Many older couples who've been devoted to each other all their lives often die within days or even hours of each other.

Chapter 2 Missing

Vocabulary

1: O | 2: S | 3: D | 4: J | 5: B | 6: F | 7: L | 8: G | 9: Q | 10: T | 11: H | 12: P | 13: N | 14: R | 15: E | 16: I | 17: M | 18: A | 19: C | 20: K

Verb tenses

1: has spent | 2: has written | 3: will emerge | 4: have occurred | 5: had been living (also: was living) | 6: had planned | 7: had left (also: left) | 8: was not | 9: was never seen | 10: heard | 11: was wearing | 12: were staying | 13: always wore | 14: took | 15: had vanished | 16: had set up | 17: wasn't getting | 18: were driving | 19: were given (also: had been given) | 20: had reported | 21: has occurred | 22: have been reported | 23: had anticipated | 24: was pulled | 25: was spotted | 26: were brought | 27: had vanished | 28: was working | 29: did not find | 30: had been headed (also: had been heading) | 31: is being perpetrated (also: has been perpetrated) | 32: do not vanish | 33: reported | 34: had lost | 35: was | 36: were left (also: had been left) | 37: were estimated | 38: have related | 39: have been eliminated | 40: was driving | 41: had set | 42: had made | 43: was trying | 44: was still playing | 45: was driving (also: had been driving) | 46: was going to be (also: would be) | 47: had hardly hung | 48: had driven | 49: had been going | 50: had been driving

A Vocabulary practice

1: tenuous | 2: Cryptographers | 3: extinction | 4: ample | 5: deserters | 6: traces | 7: abandoned | 8: clusters | 9: consumption | 10: hung up

B True / false questions

1. True | 2: False | 3: False | 4: False | 5: False | 6: False | 7: False | 8: False | 9: False | 10: False

C Sentence reconstruction

1. According to author Paulides, Yosemite National Park in California is home to the largest single cluster of unexplained disappearances.

2. The first recorded disappearance of a person from Oregon's Crater Lake was that of a photographer named Bakowski.

3. Tracking dogs are often unable to follow the scent of persons who've vanished in America's wilderness areas.

4. Police strongly suspected that the disappearance of Patrick Carnes in northern Nevada was the work of foul play.

5. People who've experienced missing time are often unable to account for their actions or whereabouts over a period of several hours.

Chapter 3 Unexplained aerial phenomena

Vocabulary

1: E | 2: H | 3: B | 4: P | 5: I | 6: O | 7: T | 8: M | 9: J | 10: N | 11: A | 12: G | 13: C | 14: F | 15: D | 16: Q | 17: S | 18: K | 19: L | 20: R

Verb tenses

1: be explained | 2: called (also: were calling *or* had been calling) | 3: were hovering (also: had been hovering) | 4: were somehow involved (also: had somehow been involved) | 5: had not been conducting (also: were not conducting) | 6: had been conducted | 7: were tracking (also: had tracked *or* had been tracking) | 8: were hovering | 9: was propelling | 10: did | 11: had witnessed (also: witnessed) | 12: gained | 13: was carrying | 14: began | 15: was flying | 16: was accompanied | 17: had gone | 18: was flying | 19: was informed | 20: did | 21: was told (also: had been told) | 22: noticed | 23: were tracking | 24: continued | 25: rearranged | 26: knew | 27: were seeing | 28: were emanating | 29: emitted | 30: jumped | 31: knew | 32: were being sighted | 33: had remained (also: remained) | 34: were forced (also: had been forced) | 35: were picking | 36: were seeking (also: sought) | 37: were telling | 38: neared | 39: picked (also: were picking) | 40: were seeing | 41: is | 42: does not have | 43: were interviewed | 44: described | 45: looked | 46: had tailed | 47: were later analyzed | 48: are displayed | 49: likely mean | 50: will remain

A Vocabulary practice

1: intruders | 2: intend | 3: novel | 4: altitude | 5: picking up | 6: brightly | 7: walks of life | 8: stacked | 9: minuscule | 10: took (take) place

B True / false questions

1: False | 2: False | 3: False | 4: False | 5: False | 6: False | 7: True | 8: True | 9: False | 10: False

C Sentence reconstruction

1. The large numbers of UFOs over Belgium in the late 1980s were seen by people from all walks of life.

2. The Belgian UFOs were tracked by multiple military radar sources.

3. The flight crew of JAL 1628 were visibly shaken by the appearance of three large UFOs that tracked their plane over Alaska in November of 1986.

4. The UFOs reported by JAL 1628 were confirmed by both military and civilian radar.

5. The UFOs that were witnessed by Belgian fighter pilots displayed flight patterns that would be impossible for humanly engineered aircraft.

Chapter 4 Off-Limits

Vocabulary

1: H | 2: K | 3: B | 4: F | 5: J | 6: G | 7: M | 8: I | 9: P | 10: T | 11: O | 12: R | 13: C | 14: E | 15: A | 16: D | 17: N | 18: L | 19: Q | 20: S

Verb tenses

1: lies | 2: became (also: have become) | 3: were released | 4: denied | 5: is kept | 6: identify (also: identified) | 7: are conducted (also: are being conducted) | 8: is run | 9: are flown | 10: forced | 11: were represented | 12: testified | 13: had been seriously sickened | 14: were working | 15: contended | 16: had died | 17: was (also: had been) | 18: had not acted (also: had not been acting) | 19: rejected | 20: persuaded | 21: guards | 22: scurry | 23: lead | 24: are quickly met | 25: warn | 26: has led | 27: was once employed (also: had once been employed) | 28: had somehow obtained | 29: be corroborated | 30: are made

A Vocabulary practice

1: lawsuit | 2: off-limits | 3: comply | 4: surroundings | 5: disclose | 6: select | 7: civilians | 8: negligence | 9: pertinent | 10: restrict

B True / false questions

1: True | 2: True | 3: False | 4: False | 5: False | 6: False | 7: False | 8: True | 9: False | 10: False

C Sentence reconstruction

1. Operated by the U.S. government, Area 51 is one of the most secretive and heavily guarded places on earth.

2. The work or research conducted at Area 51 is so highly classified that employees must be flown in on unmarked airplanes.

3. Former employees at Area 51 who became gravely ill as a result of their work there sued the U.S. Air Force for exposing them to highly toxic substances.

4. Former president Clinton issued an executive determination exempting Area 51 from compliance with federal environmental regulations.

5. Signs outside the perimeter of Area 51 warn unwelcome visitors that the use of deadly force is authorized.

Chapter 5 The Mystery of Malaysian MH370

Vocabulary

1: D | 2: G | 3: A | 4: P | 5: T | 6: O | 7: H | 8: M | 9: I | 10: E | 11: B | 12: Q | 13: K | 14: L | 15: N | 16: F | 17: C | 18: R | 19: J | 20: S

Verb tenses

1: was carrying | 2: were returning | 3: have taken | 4: had reached | 5: had appeared (also: appeared) | 6: attempted | 7: had managed | 8: turned | 9: headed | 10: was hugging (also: hugged) | 11: contacted | 12: had disappeared | 13: started (also: was started) | 14: had taken | 15: had flown | 16: had not sent | 17: had crossed | 18: made | 19: approached | 20: flew | 21: had been intentionally switched | 22: repeatedly sent (also: was repeatedly sending / had repeatedly sent) | 23: received (also with 'was repeatedly sending': receiving) | 24: continued (also: had continued) | 25: ran | 26: searched | 27: had had | 28: were forced | 29: were | 30: washed | 31: were working (also: had been working) | 32: indeed went (also: had indeed gone) | 33: were | 34: be found | 35: provided | 36: believed | 37: turned (also: had turned) | 38: headed | 39: fit (or British: fitted) | 40: wanted (also: had wanted / was wanting) | 41: had been (also: was) | 42: accomplished | 43: confirmed | 44: had been investigating (also: was investigating) | 45: had provided | 46: had practiced (also: had been practicing)

A Vocabulary practice

1. distress | 2: static | 3: suicide | 4: detect | 5: debris | 6: headed back | 7: chilling | 8: incoherent | 9: avoid | 10: mumbled

B True / false questions

1. False | 2: False | 3: False | 4: False | 5: False | 6: False | 7: False | 8: True | 9: False | 10: True

C Sentence reconstruction

1. MH370 reached its cruising altitude approximately 20 minutes after takeoff.

2. MH370 briefly entered Vietnamese airspace before inexplicably reversing course and heading back southwest over the Malaysian peninsula.

3. The majority of the passengers on board MH370 were Chinese nationals heading back home.

4. International search and rescue teams could not understand why MH370 had flown so far off its scheduled flight plan.

5. The pilot of MH370 had reportedly practiced on his home computer almost the exact route the plane is believed to have taken.

Chapter 6 Mystery in the Ural Mountains

Vocabulary

1: N | 2: R | 3: M | 4: G | 5: K | 6: Q | 7: O | 8: C | 9: J | 10: A | 11: P | 12: L | 13: T | 14: H | 15: D | 16: F | 17: E | 18: I | 19: B | 20: S

Verb tenses

1: has ever been given | 2: had been planned | 3: missed (also: had missed) | 4: set | 5: took | 6: agreed (also: had agreed) | 7: had originally planned | 8: began | 9: had not heard | 10: sent | 11: had taken | 12: arrived | 13: were still standing | 14: had been cut | 15: discovered | 16: was lying | 17: had been found (also: were found) | 18: had melted (also: melted) | 19:

located | 20: had built | 21: had first discovered | 22: were performed | 23: had suffered | 24: had been removed | 25: had still been | 26: was also attributed | 27: have knocked | 28: did not fit | 29: was covered | 30: had | 31: was singed | 32: was wearing | 33: exhibited | 34: was missing | 35: have forced | 36: have kept | 37: had obviously left | 38: were wearing | 39: have been advanced | 40: caused | 41: does not explain | 42: was | 43: were sustained (also: had been sustained) | 44: posits | 45: set (also: had set) | 46: has ever occurred | 47: were killed | 48: were attacked | 49: were seen | 50: have been proposed

A Vocabulary practice

1. wilderness | 2: bruise | 3: perplexed | 4: notified | 5: expeditions (also possible: treks) | 6: bring about | 7: gorges | 8: melting | 9: oddly | 10: volunteers

B True / false questions

1. False | 2: False | 3: False | 4: False | 5: False | 6: True | 7: False | 8: False | 9: False | 10: False

C Sentence reconstruction

1. The nine men and women who met their tragic demise in the Ural Mountains in 1959 were all young, experienced skiers and hikers.

2. Investigators still cannot explain why some of the Dyatlov team members cut open their own tents from the inside.

3. A number of the deceased hikers were found scantily dressed with only socks on their feet.

4. The eyes and tongue had been removed from one of the female hikers.

5. Autopsies revealed that most of the victims had died of hypothermia.

Chapter 7 The Bilderberg Group

Vocabulary

1: E | 2: I | 3: C | 4: A | 5: F | 6: Q | 7: T | 8: K | 9: P | 10: J | 11: O | 12: H | 13: D | 14: S | 15: N | 16: L | 17: M | 18: B | 19: R | 20: G

Verb tenses

1. meets | 2: brings | 3: remain | 4: are not allowed | 5: are admitted | 6: take | 7: are usually held | 8: are restricted | 9: derives (also: is derived) | 10: took | 11: walks | 12: are organized | 13: is sent | 14: are drawn | 15: is chaired | 16: has been | 17: was previously held | 18:

pulls | 19: include (also: included) | 20: have wondered | 21: ignore | 22: gathered | 23: huddle | 24: is easily explained | 25: are asked | 26: consider | 27: keep | 28: consistently argue (also: have consistently argued) | 29: create | 30: worries | 31: sets | 32: be judged | 33: has followed | 34: describes (also: described *or* has described) | 35: listed (also: lists *or* has listed) | 36: goes | 37: sit | 38: are magically appointed | 39: has been gleaned | 40: stands | 41: is also called (also: has also been called) | 42: has written (also: wrote) | 43: have been told | 44: are designing | 45: implementing | 46: is | 47: have learned | 48: answer | 49: believe | 50: allow

A Vocabulary practice

1: frank | 2: diligently | 3: nefarious | 4. protocol | 5: oversight | 6: conglomerates | 7: detained | 8: conscientious | 9: dominated | 10: paternalistic

B True / false questions

1: False | 2: True | 3: True | 4: False | 5: False | 6: True | 7: False | 8: False | 9: False | 10: False

C Sentence reconstruction

1. The Bilderberg brings together some of the most powerful men and women in the West for meetings once per year.

2. The Bilderberg Group adheres strictly to secrecy protocols that forbid any recordings or communication with the press or outside world.

3. Venues for Bilderberg are always securely guarded by the host country's police and military forces.

4. For many years, Western media completely ignored the existence of Bilderberg.

5. Bilderberg members have been accused of planning and plotting the courses of nations without the consent or even knowledge of the governed.

Chapter 8 Our Mysterious Universe

Vocabulary

1: I | 2: M | 3: O | 4: A | 5: F | 6: D | 7: J | 8: R | 9: T | 10: Q | 11: B | 12: E | 13: G | 14: L | 15: N | 16: K | 17: H | 18: P | 19: S | 20: C

Verb tenses

1: posit | 2: hold | 3: came | 4: went | 5: brought | 6: are | 7: see | 8: is affectionately known | 9: inflated | 10: became | 11: see | 12: had previously debated | 13: pull | 14: will fly | 15: leads | 16: will overcome | 17: began | 18: were obtained | 19: has been proceeding | 20: knows | 21: is happening | 22: will eventually recede | 23: will escape | 24: seems | 25: started | 26: haven't been | 27: date | 28: causes | 29: imply | 30: holds | 31: is made | 32: looks | 33: don't need | 34: sees | 35: content | 36: exist | 37: became | 38: have contributed

A Vocabulary practice

1: monotheistic | 2: fate | 3: simultaneously | 4: relentless | 5: exponentially | 6: noble | 7: infinitesimally | 8: outcome | 9: trigger | 10: elegant

B True / false questions

1: False | 2: False | 3: True | 4: False | 5: False | 6: True | 7: False | 8: True | 9: False | 10: False

C Sentence Reconstruction

1. The cosmological theory of inflation posits that the entire universe entered an incomprehensibly rapid phase of expansion immediately after the Big Bang.

2. Current observations indicate that the universe is expanding at an increasing rate.

3. According to the Copenhagen interpretation of quantum mechanics, quantum events are not "decided" until an observer actually looks.

4. In the many worlds interpretation, all possible outcomes of all possible events exist simultaneously.

5. The theory of multiverses allows for the continual birth and death of a potentially endless series of universes.

Chapter 9 Apparitions

Vocabulary

1: S | 2: F | 3: A | 4: P | 5: D | 6: M | 7: Q | 8: C | 9: G | 10: I | 11: R | 12: T | 13: L | 14: K | 15: E | 16: B | 17: H | 18: N | 19: J | 20: O

Verb tenses

1: have had | 2: have occurred | 3: has been handed | 4: routinely made | 5: is still sold (or: still is sold) | 6: exhibits | 7: reacts | 8: allows | 9: was exposed | 10: are recorded | 11: be altered | 12: have been attempted | 13: was taken | 14: had been killed | 15: was taken | 16: was developed | 17: recognized | 18: was standing | 19: was ever taken | 20: was waiting (or: had been waiting) | 21: ministered | 22: have not been spared | 23: was | 24: woke | 25: witnessed | 26: have been reported | 27: broke | 28: set | 29: always travelled | 30: collided | 31: struggled | 32: retired (also: was retired) | 33: were dressed | 34: have not been used | 35: was being torn | 36: have sounded | 37: have also stated | 38: was originally designed | 39: has also been seen | 40: heard (also: had heard) | 41: has not been used | 42: has ever been provided | 43: have had | 44: will likely remain

A Vocabulary practice

1: graves | 2: depth of field | 3: emulsions | 4: spectrum | 5: darkrooms | 6: altar | 7: apertures | 8: fidelity | 9: propeller | 10: substrates

B True / false questions

1: False | 2: False | 3: False | 4: False | 5: True | 6: False | 7: False | 8: True | 9: False | 10: True

C Sentence Reconstruction

1. No photographic evidence has ever been provided that proves the existence of ghosts.

2. Both staff members and hotel guests on board the *Queen Mary* have reported seeing apparitions that no one can yet explain.

3. The sinking of the *Curacao* was ultimately attributed to human error.

4. Numerous guests who have spent the night in the White House have reported seeing the ghost of Lincoln.

5. Because photographic images can always be edited and manipulated, it is difficult to see how a picture could ever offer proof of the existence of UFOs or ghosts.

Appendix

Review of Active Verb Tenses

PRESENT SYSTEM

Simple Present

Declarative sentence: *Flight 101 to London departs at 15:30.*

Negative: *My instructor doesn't come to school on Fridays.*

Wh-question: *Where does your father work?*

Yes / No question: *Do you like spaghetti?*

Present Progressive

Declarative sentence: *We are painting our kitchen yellow.*

Negative: *The children aren't listening to you.*

Wh-question: *Why is he pretending to be Italian?*

Yes / No question: *Are you using this computer now?*

Present Perfect

Declarative sentence: *Judith has just completed her medical degree.*

Negative: *We haven't seen the director all day.*

Wh-question: *What have you done to your hair?*

Yes / No question: *Have you ever been to Cairo?*

Present Perfect Progressive

Declarative sentence: *Lucy has been studying Mandarin in Beijing for the last six months.*

Negative: *I haven't been sleeping very well the last few nights.*

Wh-question: *What have you been doing since the last time we saw each other?*

Yes / No question: *Have you been watching the new mystery series on Channel 4?*

PAST SYSTEM

Past Simple

Declarative sentence: *Luigi taught English in Rome.*

Negative: *Alice didn't eat anything for breakfast this morning.*

Wh-question: *Where did you learn to play the violin?*

Yes / No question: *Did you attend any concerts at Royal Albert Hall?*

Past Progressive

Declarative sentence: *Philip was working from 7 until well after midnight last night*

Negative: *The two brothers weren't talking to each other during dinner.*

Wh-question: *Why was your husband sleeping on the couch last night?*

Yes / No question: *Were you listening to Sibelius earlier this evening?*

Past Perfect

Declarative sentence: *Elizabeth had already mastered Latin and Greek by the time she finished middle school.*

Negative: *Joe hadn't eaten anything before his birthday dinner.*

Wh-question: *How much had the twins already spent before their parents cut off their allowance?*

Yes / No question: *Had Julia already divorced her husband before she started dating again?*

Past Perfect Progressive

Declarative sentence: *Jim had already been swimming for more than two hours by the time we got to the pool.*

Negative: *The Garcias hadn't been living in California for more than two weeks before the earthquake struck.*

Wh-question: *Where had Carrie been working before she signed on with IBM?*

Yes / No question: *Had you already been performing regularly before you became a professional soloist?*

FUTURE SYSTEM

Future Simple

Declarative sentence: *My sister will help you with your redecorating project.*

Negative: *We won't have time to visit Crater Lake this summer.*

Wh-question: *What will they do without any money?*

Yes / No question: *Will you come to our wedding?*

Future Progressive

Declarative sentence: *Our company CEO will be touring through Oman next summer.*

Negative: *Unfortunately, we won't be attending any opera performances during our trip to Milan.*

Wh-question: *How will you be celebrating your tenth anniversary?*

Yes / No question: *Will Jun be focusing on climate change during his talk at the conference?*

Future Perfect

Declarative sentence: *By closing time, George will have written over 100 emails.*

Negative: *Most of the guests will not have seen your magic tricks before, I'm sure.*

Wh-question: *Will you have completed all the required courses by May?*

Yes / No question: *Won't you soon have earned enough to buy that new car you want?*

Future Perfect Progressive

Declarative sentence: *Kenji will soon have been working at the company for 25 years.*

Negative: *Even by the end of this year, Antonio won't have been studying long enough to qualify for a degree.*

Wh-question: *How long will Pjotr have been working by the time he retires?*

Yes / No question: *Will you have been living in Switzerland long enough to qualify for a work permit next year?*

Common Collocations of Verbs + Prepositions

VERBS + about

ARGUE

My colleagues were arguing about two political candidates all during dinner last night.

BE CONCERNED

The students aren't at all concerned about their low test scores.

BE WORRIED

I'm very worried about my aunt's heart problems; she's headed for bypass surgery yet again.

BOAST

Greg is always boasting about how much money he makes.

BRAG

I honestly can't endure people who brag about how much they own and how much money they earn.

CARE

Carlos seems to care too much about the opinions of other people.

CRY

There's no use crying about the money you lost in the slot machines. It's gone now and it's not coming back.

DREAM

Last night, I dreamed about a very difficult calculus exam I had in high school.

FRET

Many poor families fret constantly about how they can feed and clothe their children.

PROTEST

Students have been protesting about the massive increases in tuition fees that were recently approved.

RANT

My choleric boss was ranting on and on about the excessive coffee consumption at work.

SCREAM

My neighbor was screaming about the cars that were illegally blocking her garage.

TALK

Jean and Joan must have been talking about something very private because they both stopped talking immediately when they saw me.

WORRY

My neighbor is very worried about her son's low grades in school.

VERBS + against

ARGUE

Many financial advisers would argue against taking out a home equity loan with the prospect of higher interest rates on the horizon.

COUNT

Coming to work drunk two days in a row is definitely going to count against you in terms of merit pay.

INSURE

In almost all coastal cities, home owners must have their property insured against flooding and wind damage.

PROTEST

Students are protesting against the latest military involvement in the Middle East.

VERBS + at

GLANCE

Sarah quickly glanced at her phone to see what time it was before leaving for work.

GLARE

The diplomat just glared at the underling for spilling wine on the visiting ambassador.

GUESS

The cars were lined up literally bumper to bumper, so we could only guess at how long it was going to take us to get out of town.

HINT

My boyfriend was hinting at how much weight he thought I'd gained.

LOOK

Suzanne was looking at her bank statements when I walked into the room.

MARVEL

The entire audience marveled at the oboist's virtuosity.

SUCCEED

Gifted artists often succeed at creating masterpieces without even really studying the trade.

VERBS + for

ACCOUNT

We don't know of any concrete experiences that could account for Martha's unusually aggressive behavior.

ALLOW

Strict university policies do not allow for the admission of students with IELTS scores below 7.

APOLOGIZE

Antonio apologized several times for his rude behavior.

BARGAIN

Thomas decided to take up corporate law, but in the end the mountains of work turned out to be far more than he had bargained for.

BLAME

The managers blamed the poor single mother of three for taking too many family leave days.

CARE

Victoria is having to care for her ailing parents, both of whom can no longer walk on their own.

CHARGE

Unfortunately, we'll have to charge you for the items you broke during the party last week.

COUNT

Punctuality and reliability count for a great deal in my book.

EARMARK

Conservative lawmakers have earmarked millions for offshore drilling projects.

PAY

The Smiths actually asked us to pay for the coffee we drank while staying with them last weekend.

SELL

Vivian Maier's iconic fine art images are selling for a small fortune these days.

VERBS + from

BAR

The witness was barred from the courtroom after he threatened the judge and the jury.

BENEFIT

Most people will benefit greatly from even a moderate amount of daily exercise.

DIFFER

The clarinet differs significantly from the oboe because the latter requires two reeds whereas the former requires only one.

DISTINGUISH

Only trained gemologists can distinguish natural diamonds from top-quality synthetic ones.

DISTRACT

Many young people today are routinely distracted from both their studies and the entire world around them by the constant beckoning of social media.

EXEMPT

In many countries, a serious medical condition will exempt you from mandatory jury duty.

EXPEL

At the end of 2016, the Obama administration expelled 35 Russian diplomats from the USA.

REFRAIN

We kindly ask you to refrain from talking or using any electronic devices during the performance.

RESIGN

We have asked the party chairperson to resign from her position immediately because of the scandalous material that has recently come to light.

RESULT

Type II diabetes often results from obesity and a long-term excess intake of carbohydrates, such as refined grain products and sweets.

STEM

Increased extinction rates among many animal species stem from the uncontrolled growth of human habitations.

SUFFER

Many elderly people suffer from degenerative diseases such as osteoarthritis.

VERBS + in

BE

I drove by my cousin's house last night be she wasn't in when I got there.

BE ABSORBED

Marjorie was so absorbed in the crossword puzzle she was working on that she didn't even hear the phone ring.

BE ENGROSSED

Weihan was so engrossed in his computer game that he didn't realize the lights had gone out.

CONFIDE

I've known my closest friend so long I know I can confide anything in him.

INVOLVE

The husband and wife are trying not to involve their kids in any of their frequent marital disputes.

MAJOR

My niece is majoring in theoretical physics at Cambridge.

RESULT

Your failure to respond to our requests for more information may result in the cancellation of your contract.

SPECIALIZE

My wife is specializing in climate studies.

SUCCEED

Still to this day, science has not succeeded in developing an effective vaccine against all strains of the common cold.

VERBS + of

ACCUSE

Three prominent party members are being accused of embezzlement.

CONVICT

Julius and Ethel Rosenberg were convicted of espionage in the service of the former Soviet Union.

CURE

Daily consumption of aloe vera juice seems to have cured James of his ulcers.

DIE

Actor Debbie Reynolds literally died of the extreme grief she felt one day after the passing of her daughter, Carrie Fisher.

SUSPECT

Former energy giant was suspected of cooking the books to make the company's overall market value look much better than it actually was.

VERBS + on

BASE

The prosecution based its case on nothing more than hearsay and flimsy circumstantial evidence.

BE BASED

Many believed that the accusations leveled against the Russian government for tampering with U.S. elections in 2016 were based on nothing more than propaganda and rumors.

BLAME

Someone put glue on the doors of the boss's car and everyone blamed the incident on me.

CENTER

Eoj's new advertising strategy centers on everyday forms of humor.

CONCENTRATE

The company's research and development division is currently concentrating on devices that interface with clients' mood swings.

CONGRATULATE

The board of directors has congratulated us on surpassing our performance goals this year by leaps and bounds.

DECIDE

Have you already decided on a name for your baby?

ELABORATE

Would you care to elaborate on the characters in and settings for your new novel?

IMPOSE

We really don't want to impose on you, but would you be able to put us up for two nights?

INSIST

The director of our department insists on everyone always being on time for meetings.

SIT

The government sat on the very negative data and prayed that it would never come to light.

WORK

Leading German optical companies are now working on lenses that will resolve up to 1000 lines per millimeter.

VERBS + to

AMOUNT

Your children will never amount to anything if they don't learn self-discipline.

ANSWER

The wonderful thing about being your own boss is that you don't have to answer to anyone except yourself.

APPEAL

Somehow the idea of vacationing in the Arctic just doesn't appeal to me at all.

APPLY

The new tax laws do not apply to those earning only the minimum wage.

ATTRIBUTE

The rise in business bankruptcies can be attributed to the liquidity crisis in the banking system.

BE USED

Teresa is not used to getting up before dawn.

CATER

The company's new software caters to people who are not particularly computer savvy.

COMMIT

The couple have committed an abundance of time and money to improving their community.

CONFESS

The two thieves didn't confess to the robbery until they were confronted with the CCTV footage in which they were clearly visible.

CONTRIBUTE

Writing longhand as opposed to typing has been shown to contribute to much greater creativity and a higher order of verbal skills.

DEVOTE

Performance musicians must devote all their time and energy to mastering the respective repertoire for their instruments.

PREFER

True recluses most often prefer to spend their time at home away from public crowds.

REACT

The company's press office has not reacted to the latest allegations of misconduct by the firm's CEO.

REFER

In my letter to the local utilities commission, I referred to growing public discontent with the unreliability of services.

RESORT

If the neighbors continue behaving in such an uncivil manner, we'll have to resort to legal action.

SEE

Could you see to our garden while we're on vacation?

SUBJECT

We were subjected to rough, unacceptable behavior at the hands of the security guards.

TALK

People who find themselves trapped in prolonged depression often benefit by having someone close to talk to.

VERBS + with

ACQUAINT

I definitely need to better acquaint myself with all the culture that Edinburgh has to offer.

ARGUE

There's really no point trying to argue with Bonnie; she's as stubborn as a mule.

ASSOCIATE

Personally, I would never associate with someone with a violent past.

BE CONCERNED

My adviser doesn't want to be concerned with collecting the data herself; she prefers to conduct the final analysis.

BE FACED

Our government is faced with an astronomical budget deficit.

CHARGE

Two men from Nebraska have been charged with breaking into the Pentagon's computer system.

CLASH

Rioters clashed with police outside government headquarters.

COINCIDE

Two remarkable celestial events coincide with special religious holidays this year.

COLLIDE

Seven automobiles collided with two large trucks on the A7 motorway this week.

COMPLY

Tenants who refuse to comply with the new noise regulations will be served with eviction notices.

CONFRONT

We don't want to confront Geoffrey with these allegations until we have irrefutable proof that they're true.

CONFUSE

Many people routinely confuse the oboe with the clarinet because of their similar shape, color, and size.

DEAL

I find it very challenging to deal with people who are overtly aggressive.

FILL

If you want to take a nice bath, I'll fill the tub with hot water.

MEET

Representatives from the unions are meeting with our staff later this week.

PLEAD

Janet's parents are pleading with her to give up skydiving.

PROVIDE

Our offices will provide you with all the assistance you need within the two-year warranty period.

TALK

We'll need to talk with the boy's teachers to see if he's able to participate in these extracurricular activities.

TAMPER

The police became suspicious the moment they realized that someone had tampered with the voting machines.

WORK

Instead of adopting a confrontational approach, it would be wiser for employees and management to try to work with each other to reach an agreeable compromise.

About the Author

JJ Polk, PhD, completed his post-doctoral teaching credentials in the UK with an UCLES Diploma. A former CELTA tutor and IELTS examiner, Polk has lived and taught in Europe, the Middle East and the Far East. He is also the author of *English Questions: Practice Drills in All Active Tenses* and *English in Global Contexts: Proficiency Tasks for Aspiring Learners.* Polk now teaches at the University of Southern California in Los Angeles and is especially interested in interdisciplinary perspectives on pragmatics in communication.

www.ingramcontent.com/pod-product-compliance
Lightning Source LLC
Chambersburg PA
CBHW082243300426
44110CB00036B/2434
* 9 7 8 0 6 9 2 8 9 2 3 7 4 *